TRUE AND FALSE

David Mamet is a writer and director. His plays include: *The Duck Variations, Sexual Perversity in Chicago, Reunion, American Buffalo, A Life in the Theatre, The Water Engine, The Woods, Prairie du Chien, Lakeboat, Edmond, The Shawl, Glengarry Glen Ross* (for which he won the Pulitzer Prize), *Speed the Plow, Bobby Gould in Hell, The Old Neighbourhood, Oleanna* and *The Cryptogram*. His screenplays include: *The Postman Always Rings Twice, The Verdict, The Untouchables, House of Games, Things Change* (with Shel Silverstein), *Homicide, Hoffa* and *Bookworm*. His collections of essays, *Writing in Restaurants, Some Freaks, On Directing Film* and *The Cabin* are published by Faber and Faber under the title of *A Whore's Profession*. His novels, *The Village, The Old Religion* and *Wilson*, are also published by Faber and Faber.

True and False

Heresy and Common Sense for the Actor

DAVID MAMET

faber and faber

First published in the USA in 1997 by Pantheon Books,
a division of Random House Inc, New York

First published in Great Britain in 1998
by Faber and Faber Limited
Bloomsbury House, 74-77 Great Russell Street,
London WCIB 3DA

Printed and bound by CPI Group (UK) Ltd, Croydon, CRO 4YY

David Mamet is hereby identified as author of this
work in accordance with Section 77 of the Copyright,
Designs and Patents Act 1988

A CIP record for this book
is available from the British Library

ISBN 978-0-571-19261-8

The scientific approach to the phenomenon of human nature enables us to be ignorant without being frightened, and without, therefore, having to invent all sorts of weird theories to explain away our gaps in knowledge.

— D. W. WINNICOTT
Towards an Objective Study of Human Nature

A magician is an actor impersonating a magician.

— JEAN EUGÈNE ROBERT-HOUDIN

CONTENTS

TRUE
AND
FALSE

TO THE ACTOR

My closest friends, my intimate companions, have always been actors. My beloved wife is an actor. My extended family consists of the actors I have grown up, worked, lived, and aged with. I have been, for many years, part of various theatre companies, any one of which in its healthy state more nearly resembles a perfect community than any other group that I have encountered.

I wanted to be an actor, but it seemed that my affections did not that way tend. I learned to write and direct so that I could stay in the theatre, and be with that company of people.

I studied acting in various schools, and could understand little of what was being said. I, and the other students, saw, I know, that the goal of the instruction was clear—to bring an immediacy to the performance—but none of us, I think, understood, nor did practice reveal, how the school's exercises were to bring that goal about.

As a teacher, director, and dramatist, I've worked—as did *my* teachers—to communicate my views to the actor. I have been fortunate in that I've had a lot of time to do it—almost thirty years—and that my views have been informed by and directed toward performance on the stage in front of a paying audience.

That is what acting is. Doing the play for the audience. The rest is just practice. And I see that the life of the academy, the graduate school, the studio, while charming and comfortable, are as removed from the life (and the job) of the actor as aerobics are from boxing.

This is a book for the actor. It contains, I hope, a little common sense, and a few basic principles. I hope that they will aid you to appreciate, to understand, to practice, this most challenging, and most worthy of endeavors.

SOME THOUGHTS

As actors, we spend most of our time nauseated, confused, guilty. We are lost and ashamed of it; confused because we don't know what to do and we have too much information, none of which can be acted upon; and guilty because we feel we are not doing our job. We feel we have not learned our job well enough; we feel others know *their* job but we have failed. The good we do seems to be through chance: if only that agent would notice me; if only that producer had come on Tuesday night when I was good rather than on Wednesday night when I was off; if only the script allowed me to do more *this* and less *that*; if only the audience had been better; if only we had not gone up five minutes late—as a consequence of which I lost my concentration.

So we become envious of those who have "luck," of those who, seemingly, have "technique," as, having no "technique" ourselves, we think that their accomplishments must be based on "luck." So we invest more heavily in a "technique based on luck," and it becomes, in effect, a *superstition*, an investment in self-consciousness, in introversion. We turn our attention inward because introversion spares us from the horrible necessity of living in a theatre world for which we are totally unprepared. So our "technique" becomes more and more devoted to the development of a kind of catatonia: Sense memory. Substitution. Emotional memory. The "Fourth Wall." The creation of auxiliary "stories" which are just as difficult to "perform" as the script but lack the merit of being about anything other than ourselves.

The Stanislavsky "Method," and the technique of the schools derived from it, is nonsense. It is not a technique out of the practice of which one develops a skill—it is a cult. The organic demands made on the actor are much more compelling, and the potential accomplishments of the actor much more important—the life and work, if I may say so, much more heroic—than anything prescribed or foreseen by this or any other "method" of acting.

Acting is not a genteel profession. Actors used to be buried at a crossroads with a stake through the heart. Those people's performances so troubled the onlookers that they feared their ghosts. An awesome compliment. Those players moved the audience not such that they were admitted to a graduate school, or received a complimentary review, but such that the audience feared for their soul. Now that seems to me something to aim for.

Here are some thoughts on the subject.

ANCESTOR WORSHIP

Stanislavsky was essentially an amateur. He was a member of a very wealthy merchant family, and he came to the theatre as a rich man. I do not mean to denigrate either his fervor or his accomplishments—I merely note his antecedents.

The busker, the gypsy, the mountebank, come to the theatre to support themselves. As their support depends directly upon the favor of the audience, they study to obtain that favor. Those who have, in the perhaps overused phrase, "come up from the streets," have little interest in their own performance, save as it relates to their ability to please an audience. This is, I believe, as it should be.

I do not assume that the doctor, or the musician or dancer or painter, strives first to bring himself to a "state," and only then directs his efforts outward. I assume that practitioners of these crafts put their attention on the legitimate demands of their profession and of their clients; and I, as a client, patient, audience member, do not expect these professionals to burden me with their life story.

The actor is onstage to communicate the play to the audience. That is the beginning and the end of his and her job. To do so the actor needs a strong voice, superb diction, a supple, well-proportioned body, and a rudimentary understanding of the play.

The actor does not need to "become" the character. The phrase, in fact, has no meaning. There *is* no character. There are only lines upon a page. They are lines of dialogue meant to be said by the actor. When he or she says them simply, in an attempt to achieve an object more or less like that suggested by the author, the audience sees an *illusion* of a character upon the stage.

To create this illusion the actor has to undergo nothing whatever. He or she is as free of the necessity of "feeling" as the magician is free of the necessity of actually summoning supernormal powers. The magician creates an illusion in the mind of the audience. So does the actor.

Eisenstein wrote that the true power of film came from the synthesis *in the mind of the viewer* of shot A and shot B: e.g., shot A, a teakettle whistling; shot B, a young woman raises her head from a desk. The viewer is thus given the idea "rising to renewed labors." If shot A is a black-robed judge being handed an envelope, he opens it, and clears his throat; and shot B is the same as before—a woman raising her head from a desk—the audience creates the idea "hearing the verdict."

The action of the woman is the same in each case, her snippet of film is the same. Nothing has changed except the juxtaposition of images, but that juxtaposition gives the audience a completely new idea.

Eisenstein theorizes, and I believe his theory is borne out in example, that the idea so created is *vastly* stronger—i.e., more effective—than simply "following the protagonist around"—i.e., using the *camera* to tell the story rather than using the cut; that this method of storytelling is superior because it is the viewer who creates the idea—who, in effect, tells herself the story.

Similarly, it is the juxtaposition in the mind of the audience between the spoken word of the author and the simple directed-but-uninflected action of the actor which creates the ineluctable idea of character in the mind of the audience.

———

Most acting training is directed at recapitulating the script. Actors are told to learn how to "be happy," "be sad," "be distracted," at those points in the script or performance where it would seem the "character" would so be. Such behavior is not only unnecessary, it is harmful both to the actor and to the audience.

My philosophical bent and thirty years' experience inform me that nothing in the world is less interesting than an actor on the stage involved in his or her own emotions. The very act of striving to create an emotional state in oneself takes one out of the play. It is the ultimate self-consciousness, and though it may be self-consciousness in the service of an ideal, it is no less boring for that.

The actor on the stage, looking for or striving to create a "state" in himself can think only one of two things: (a) I have not reached the required state yet; I am deficient and must try harder; or (b) I *have* reached the required state, how proficient I am! (at which point the mind, ever jealous of its prerogatives, will reduce the actor to (a).

Both (a) and (b) take the actor right out of the play. For the mind cannot be forced. It can be suggested, but it cannot be forced. An actor onstage can no more act upon the order "Be happy" than she can upon the order "Do not think of a hippopotamus."

Our emotional-psychological makeup is such that our only response to an order to think or feel anything is rebellion. Think of the times someone suggested that you "cheer up," of the perfect young person your friends wanted to fix you up with, of the director who suggested you "relax." The response to an emotional demand is antagonism and rebellion. There is no exception. If one were truly able to command one's conscious thoughts, to summon emotion at will, there would be no neurosis, no psychosis, no psychoanalysis, no sadness.

We cannot control our thoughts, nor can we control our emotions. But perhaps "control of emotion" has a special case-specific meaning upon the stage. Indeed it does. It means "pretending."

I don't care to see a musician concentrating on what he or she feels while performing. Nor do I care to see an actor do so. As a playwright and as a lover of good writing, I know that the good play does not *need* the support of the actor, in effect, narrating its psychological undertones, and that the bad play will not benefit from it.

"Emotional memory," "sense memory," and the tenets of the Method back to and including Stanislavsky's trilogy are a lot of hogwash. This "method" does not work; it cannot be practiced; it is, in theory, design, and supposed execution supererogatory—it is as useless as teaching pilots to flap their arms while in the cockpit in order to increase the lift of the plane.

The plane is designed to fly; the pilot is trained to direct it. Likewise, the play is designed, if correctly designed, as a series of incidents in which and through which the protagonist struggles toward his or her goal. It is the job of the actor to show up, and use the lines and his or her will and common sense, to attempt to achieve a goal similar to that of the protagonist. And that is the end of the actor's job.

In "real life" the mother begging for her child's life, the criminal begging for a pardon, the atoning lover pleading for one last chance—these people give no attention *whatever* to their own state, and all attention to the state of that person from whom they require their object. This outward-directedness brings the actor in "real life" to a state of magnificent responsiveness and makes his progress thrilling to watch.

On the stage, similarly, it is the progress of the outward-directed actor, who behaves with no regard to his personal state, but with *all* regard for the responses of his antagonists, which thrills the viewers. Great drama, onstage or off, is not the performance of deeds with great emotion, but the performance of great deeds with no emotion whatever.

Now, will the outward-directed actor not be, now and again, "moved"? Certainly, as will anyone in any circumstance, giving all of his or her attention to a task—but this emotion is a by-product, and a trivial by-product, of the performance of the action. It is not the point of the exercise. The bogus politician strives for verisimilitude. Roosevelt, on December 7, 1941, had more important things to do.

―――

The simple performance of the great deed, onstage or off, is called "heroism." The person who will not be swayed, who perseveres no matter what—that hero has the capacity to inspire us, to suggest that we reexamine our self-imposed limitations and try again.

In politics, in sport, at work, or in literature, that hero suggests through selflessness that we can be better than we are. The liar, the pretender, the self-promoter, the false performer full of crocodile tears, jingoism, cheap patriotism—that person may compel our admiration for a moment, but will subsequently leave us unsure, angry, and degraded.

Similarly, onstage, the Great Actor, capable of bringing herself to tears, may extort our admiration for her "accomplishment," but she will never leave us stronger; she has made us pay a price, and made us pretend we like it, but we leave the theatre moved only by our capacity to be moved.

Well, then, how did the Method "greats" rise to prominence, if not through their studies?

Through the gifts which God gave them, through experience, and in spite of their studies—to quote Fielding, "Education being proved useless save in those cases where it is almost superfluous."

Actors almost without exception pursue a course of study. As all have passed through *some* "training," and as a small but predictable percentage of them will have been graced with a predisposition for the stage, therefore a small percentage will reflect glory on *some* institution. I suggest, though, that there is no cause-and-effect relationship—it is as if Corsica, claiming Napoleon, recommended herself as a training ground for emperors.

And, of course, the Actors' Studio, in the fifties, arrogated to itself some fine talents. The Studio, however, *chose* them; it did not *make* them. The best actors, passing through a rigorous and extensive auditioning process, were admitted to the Studio—an admittance deemed a great honor. Why would the Studio, and why should the actor, demean the operations of instruction? Administrative self-interest and filial piety would insure that they would not; but I suggest that they, the accomplished actors, young, vital, talented, and hearty, succeeded and succeed, at the Studio and elsewhere, *in spite of* their training.

Stanislavsky was certainly a master administrator, may have been a brilliant director and/or actor, and was widely heralded as a theoretician. But I say that his contribution as a theoretician was that of a dilettante, and has, since his day, been a lodestone for the theoretical, I will say the *anti*practical, soul. For amateurs. For his theories cannot be put into practice.

Like their coeval harness-mate, psychoanalysis, they can demand fealty and long-term devotion, but they rarely, if ever, show demonstrable results. Again like psychoanalysis, they command the time and attention of many who would otherwise be hard put to fill an idle hour; and, to complete the conceit, they, neither of them, tend toward closure, i.e., a completion of a course of action/study—for such closure would deprive the devotee of an enjoyable occupation.

The professional performs for pay. Her job is to play the piece such that the audience may understand it— the self-respecting person keeps her thoughts and emotions to herself.

The paint-by-numbers dissection of the play into emotional oases is the hobbyhorse of those whom
chance or mischance has freed of the necessity to make
their living on the stage.

A GENERATION
THAT WOULD LIKE TO STAY IN SCHOOL

You ou readers are of a generation that would like to stay in school. The world is, as usual, a frightening place to enter for all save the precious few impaired by inherited security. There was perhaps for a time in this country a fairly secure promise of a career for a small segment of the bourgeoisie, and now even that is gone and good grades and a little family money can no longer assure one of the sinecure in law or medicine. And further, for the player—that is, for the man or woman who is interested in a career on the stage— there never was such a security.

You will encounter in your travels folks of your own age who chose the institutional path, who became the arts administrators rather than the actors, the casting agents rather than the writers. These folks chose to serve an institutional authority in exchange for a paycheck, and these folks are going to be with you for the rest of your life, and you actors and writers and people who come up off the street, who live without certainty day to day and year to year are going to have to bear with being called children by these institutional types; you will, as Shakespeare tells us, endure "the spurns that patient merit of the unworthy takes."

It is not childish to live with uncertainty, to devote oneself to a craft rather than a career, to an idea rather than an institution. It's courageous and requires a courage of the order that the institutionally co-opted are ill equipped to perceive. They are so unequipped to perceive it that they can only call it childish, and so excuse their exploitation of you.

Part of the requirement of a life in the theatre is to stay out of school. The old joke has the young woman in her bedroom as a visitor at a castle in Transylvania when a vampire appears in the middle of the night. The young lady grabs two spoons off the night table, forms them into a cross and thrusts them at the vampire, who responds, *"Vil gurnisht Helfin,"* which is Yiddish for "It ain't gonna help." And the same is true of school.

Past vocal and physical training, and the most rudimentary instruction in script analysis—all of which, by the way, can be acquired piecemeal through observation and practice, through personal tutoring, or through a mixture of the above—such acting training will not help you. Formal education for the player is not only useless, but harmful. It stresses the academic model and denies the primacy of the interchange with the audience.

The audience will teach you how to act and the audience will teach you how to write and to direct. The classroom will teach you how to obey, and obedience in the theatre will get you nowhere. It's a soothing falsity.

Like the belief of the terminally ill in medicine, the belief of the legitimately frightened in the educational process is a comforting lie.

Young people ask if they should go to graduate school in the theatre, as they ask if it is a good idea to go to law school to improve their minds. (A question testing the limits of irony.) Alice, when in Wonderland, asked the caterpillar which road she should take, and the caterpillar responded by asking her where she wanted to end up. That's a question you might ask yourself.

If you want to be in the theatre, go into the theatre. If you want to have made a valiant effort to go into the theatre before you go into real estate or law school or marry wealth, then perhaps you should stay in school.

The skill of acting is finally a physical skill; it is not a mental exercise, and has nothing whatever to do with the ability to pass a test.

The skill of acting is not the paint-by-numbers ability to amalgamate emotional oases—to string them like pearls into a performance (the Method). Nor is it the mastery of syntax (the academic public speaking model). The skill of acting is like the skill of sport, which is a physical event. And like that endeavor, its difficulty consists to a large extent in being much simpler than it seems. Like sports, the study of acting consists in the main of getting out of one's own way, and in learning to deal with uncertainty and being comfortable being uncomfortable.

Now what do I mean by that? The Method school would teach the actor to prepare a moment, a memory, an emotion for each interchange in the play and to stick to that preparation. This is an error on the order of the basketball coach instructing his team to stick to the plays which they practiced irrespective of what their opponents are doing.

We actors, being human, do not like the unexpected. If we encounter the unexpected onstage in front of people, we are apt to reveal ourselves. And formal academic education and sense memory and emotional memory and creative "interpretation" and all of these skills which are much more appropriate, finally, to the lectern than to the stage, are ways of concealing the truth of that revelation—of that moment.

The truth of the moment is another name for what is actually happening between the two people onstage. That interchange is always unplanned, is always taking place, is always fascinating, and it is to the end of concealing that interchange that most acting training is directed.

In my earlier days actors would begin a line by adding their own words, saying "I mean." Some thought that had personalized the line and made it "more real." Today we see actors doing the same thing in a different way. It is what I call Hollywood Huff acting. The actor is given a cue, and he shuffles his feet and blows out air in a huff, much like a whale, sometimes enunciating a sort of "phew," and then continues to the assigned line. What does this mean? It means the actor was moved by an unforeseen sensation, emotion, or perception, and, in an effort to regain what he understood to be a necessary anchor of self-consciousness, he played for time. All of this happened, of course, in the merest fraction of a second, but it did happen.

And it happens all the time, that huff, that "I mean." That's where the scene went. If the actor had simply opened his mouth on cue and spoken *even though* he felt uncertain, the audience would have been treated to the truth of the moment, to a lovely, unexpected, unforeseeable beautiful exchange between the two people onstage. They would in effect have witnessed the true lost art of the actor.

Stanislavsky said that the person one is is a thousand times more interesting than the best actor one could become. And when the actor picks up her cue, then speaks out though uncertain, the audience *sees* that interesting person. They see true courage, not a portrayal of courage, but true courage. The individual onstage speaks because she is called upon to speak—when she has nothing to support her except her self-respect.

When the actual courage of the actor is coupled with the lines of the playwright, the illusion of character is created. When the audience sees the steadfastness

of the actress playing Joan coupled with the words of
Shaw, they see majesty. When they see the courage of
the actor playing Willy Loman coupled with the words
of Arthur Miller, they see anguish. And it is the cou-
pling of the truth of the actor struggling bravely with
uncertainty, with the portrayal made by the dramatist,
which, again, creates the illusion of character—the illusion of the character of the king, the murderer, or the
saint.

The Method got it wrong. Yes, the actor is undergoing something onstage, but it is beside the point to have
him or her "undergo" the supposed trials of the character upon the stage. The actor has his own trials to undergo, and they are right in front of him. They don't
have to be superadded; they exist. His challenge is not
to recapitulate, to *pretend* to the difficulties of the written
character; it is to open the mouth, stand straight, and
say the words bravely—adding nothing, denying nothing, and without the intent to manipulate anyone: himself, his fellows, the audience.

To learn to do that is to learn to act.

The actor, in learning to be true and simple, in
learning to speak to the point despite being frightened,
and with no certainty of being understood, creates his
own character; he forges character in himself. Onstage.
And it is this character which he brings to the audience,
and by which the audience is truly moved.

SCHOLARSHIP

Polite western society has long confounded scholarship with art. Scholarship is a reasoned endeavor; and the goal of scholarship, at least as it applies to the art of the actor, is to transform the scholar from a member of the audience into a being superior to it. "It is all very well," the theatrical scholars might say, "to laugh, to cry, to gasp—it's fine for the mob. But I will do something higher, and will participate only as a sort of cultural referee."

That's fine for a scholar, but for a working member of the theatre to reason thusly is to wish one's life away. Here is the taint of scholarship in the theatre: a preoccupation with *effect*. That is the misjudgment of the Method: the notion that one can determine the effect one wants to have upon an audience, and then study and supply said effect.

Preoccupation with effect is preoccupation with the self, and not only is it joyless, it's a waste of time. Can we imagine the Cockney street buskers studying what effect they wish to have on the audience at which portion of their turn? Can we imagine the African drummer doing so, the Gypsy guitarist, the klezmer? Art is an expression of joy and awe. It is not an attempt to share one's virtues and accomplishments with the audience, but an act of selfless spirit. Our effect is not for us to know. It is not in our control. Only our intention is under our control. As we strive to make our intentions pure, devoid of the desire to manipulate, and clear, directed to a concrete, easily stated end, our performances become pure and clear.

Eleven o'clock always comes. In the meantime, may you know the happiness of working to serve your own good opinion. Invent nothing, deny nothing, speak up, stand up, stay out of school.

FIND YOUR MARK

*Find your mark, look the other fellow in the eye,
and tell the truth.*

—JAMES CAGNEY

Why accept the second-rate in yourself or in others? Why laugh at the unfunny? Why sigh at the hackneyed? Why gasp at the predictable? Why do we do that? We do it because we need to laugh, to sigh, to gasp.

And in the absence of the real stimulus we are capable of being manipulated and of manipulating ourselves, to take the form for the substance. To take cheap, degraded thrills for fear of having no thrills at all. Because, remember, it is the audience that goes to the theatre to exercise its emotion—not the actor, the audience. And when they go, having paid to be moved, they exercise their right to their money's worth.

What moves them?

When we read the newspaper, we are most moved by the ordinary man or woman forced by circumstances to act in an extraordinary way. We are moved by heroism. We are not moved by the self-proclaimed emotions of the manipulative, or of the famous. We discount to the greatest extent these reports, as we fear, correctly, that they are only advertising themselves. Similarly, at the theatre or at the film, we are truly and only moved by the ordinary men or women (actors) doing their best under extraordinary circumstances, forced to act in an extraordinary way in order to achieve their goal. Just as when we read in the newspaper of the postman who rescues the invalid from the burning building. We are moved by the heroism of the ordinary person acting in an extraordinary way.

We enjoy the foibles of the great, their follies, and their self-proclamations, as it titillates both our own grandiose folly and our feeling of self-importance—as we feel ourselves, rightly, superior to them. But this thrill is cheap and it is as nothing compared to our enjoyment of real heroism. Why? Because when we see real heroism, the heroism of the ordinary person forced by circumstances to act bravely, we identify with that man or woman and we say, "If they can do it, then perhaps I could, too."

The actor who mugs, who hams it up, who lays claim to emotions which are false, or who uses these supposed emotions to make a demand upon the audience, can extort an unhappy admiration as he asks the audience in admiring him to admire itself. But the actor who tells the truth simply because the circumstances require it is like the postman who saves the invalid, the

bicycle messenger who rides in the Olympics, an ordinary man or woman behaving with address and direction in extraordinary circumstances. And, at this, we,
the audience, exercise a higher faculty than that of getting our money's worth: the faculty of admiration, of
love for true nobility in human character. Now, I have
spoken of "the situation." You say, "The postman was
placed in a situation; Hamlet was placed in a situation.
I might act *truthfully* perhaps, but cannot one act truthfully and be out of adjustment with the situation? How
can I be true to the situation?"

Stanislavsky said the actor should ask, "What would
I do in that situation?" His student Vakhtangov said the
question was more aptly put, "What must I do to do
what I would do in that situation?" But I say you should
ask not "What would I do in that situation," not "What
must I do to do what I would do in that situation?" but
you should discard the idea of "the situation" alto-
gether.

None of us has any idea whatever what we would do
in such a situation—Hamlet's or the postman's. How
can we know? Only a fool or a liar would claim to know
what they would do when called upon to act with
courage.

Well, fine then, let's disavow foreknowledge of our
capacity for bravery, for grace under pressure; and
rather than idolizing ourselves—which is what sense
memory is all about, enthroning our power to feel and
hoping that that includes the power to move—rather let

us learn to submit, as it were, to stand the gaff, to face the audience, the casting director, the opponent on the stage, with, bravely, shoulders squared. And then, rather than pretending, we can *discover* whether or not we are courageous.

Most of us, in the course of a day or a week, treat ourselves to the fantasy of the Bad News at the Doctor's Office in which we are invited to sit and hear our fate. And in that fantasy we are stoical and simple, and that is of course what makes the fantasy so pleasing to indulge in—we wait to hear the verdict on our future bravely.

Similarly onstage. The actor is placed in that position somewhere between regularly and constantly. He or she needs something the other person onstage has (in the case of the Doctor's Office fantasy it is information). The actor is given the opportunity to be brave and simple in difficult circumstances.

Here's a hint. The opportunity for bravery is always there—it is always in the play itself.

Let me explain. The actor says to himself, "I can't play this scene because I am unprepared; I can't play it because I don't like the other actor, who is a swine; I feel that the moment is wrong as the director has interpreted it; I feel this flies in the face of my preparation; the script isn't as good as I thought it was," and so on.

All of these feelings are engendered by the *script* and they are always and only engendered by the script. The fantasy that the play brings to life (the bad news from the doctor, begging for the child's life, refusing the crown) supplies everything we need to act—and all our excuses, all those supposed "impediments" to acting are, if we listen closely, merely the play asserting itself. The actor creates excuses not to act and attributes her reluctance to everything in the world except the actual cause. The play itself has brought her to life in ways she has not foreseen, and she doesn't like it one small bit. I realize this observation may seem simplistic and even Pollyannaish, and I wouldn't credit it myself except that I have seen it to be true over too long a time spent in show business.

We say, "I can't play the scene in *Hamlet* because I am unprepared, I can't play the scene in *Othello* because I don't quite trust those around me; I can't play Desdemona because I don't believe the fellow playing Othello would actually act that way. I can't play Bigger Thomas because I am furious at everyone around me. I can't play the Madame Ranyevskaya scene because I simply don't care about this project anymore."

All of the above and every other "I can't" excuse is engendered by the play because our suggestibility knows no limits. Our minds work with unbelievable speed assembling and ordering information. That is our protective device as animals, and it has enabled us both to defeat the woolly mammoth and to vote for supply-side economics—we are infinitely suggestible.

As much as we theatre folk like to think of ourselves as intellectuals, we are not. Ours is not an intellectual profession. All the book learning in the world, all the "ideas," will not enable one to play Hedda Gabler, and all the gab about the "arc of the character" and "I based my performance on . . ." is gibberish. There is no arc of the character; and one can no more base a performance on an idea than one can base a love affair on an idea. These phrases are nothing but talismans of the actor to enable him or her to ward off evil, and the evil they attempt to ward off is the terrifying unforeseen.

The magic phrases and procedures are incantations to lessen the terror of going out there naked. But that's how the actor goes out there, like it or not.

And all the emotions and sense memory and emotional checkpoints will not create certainty. On the contrary, they will only dull the actor to the one certainty onstage, which is that the moment is going to unfold as it will and in spite of the actor's desires. The actor cannot control it; he or she can only ignore it.

To return to suggestibility. The script is going to live in its own unforeseeable ways. The other people onstage will be acting in this rehearsal, in this performance, in this moment, in this take, in their own unforeseeable ways. Therefore you the actor, as you will be dealing with both the script and the others, as you are *seeing* something you did not expect, will likely be feeling something you did not expect. You will be brought to feel, as I said, "I cannot play that scene in *Hamlet* because I am unsure; I thought I understood it and now I just don't know. Also, the other actors seem to want something from me I am not in the position to deliver"—which is, of course, the same situation in which the audience discovers Hamlet—what a coincidence.

How can the actor know that that which he or she is feeling in the moment is not only acceptable but an eloquent and beautiful part of the play? The actor cannot. When onstage it's not only unnecessary but impossible to attribute one's feelings, to say, "I feel A because I am overtired, and I feel B because the 'character' should feel it, and I feel C because the fellow playing the king opposite me is a ham," and so on.

Actors like to attribute their feelings, as this gives them the illusion of control over them. Everything they try to wish away is the unexpected; which is to say again, the *play.*

The question is, how can an actor know or remember that? And the answer is, the actor can't. Time onstage moves too quickly; and the moment, if one has time to consider it, is long gone by the time the consideration begins.

So wisdom consists in this: do not attribute feelings, act on them before attributing them, before negotiating with them, before saying, "This is engendered by the play, this is not engendered by the play." Act on them.

First, although you won't believe it, they're *all* engendered by the play; and second, even if they were not, by the time you feel something, the audience has already seen it. It happened and you might as well have acted on it. (If you didn't, the audience saw not "nothing," but you, the actor, denying something.)

The above is true and it's difficult to do. It calls on the actor not to do more, not to believe more, not to work harder as part of an industrial effort, but to *act*, to speak out bravely although unprepared and frightened.

The middle-class work ethic: "But I did my preparation. It is not my fault if the truth of the moment does not conform." That ethic is not going to avail. Nobody cares how hard you worked. Nor should they.

Acting, which takes place for an audience, is not as the academic model would have us believe. It is not a test. It is an art, and it requires not tidiness, not paint-by-numbers intellectuality, but immediacy and courage.

We are of course trained in our culture to hold our tongue and control our emotions and to behave in a reasonable manner. So, to act one has to unlearn these habits, to train oneself to speak out, to respond quickly, to act forcefully, irrespective of what one feels and in so doing to create the habit, not of "understanding," not of "attributing," the moment, but of giving up control and, in so doing, giving oneself up to the play.

Acting in my lifetime has grown steadily away from performance and toward what for want of a better term can only be called oral interpretation, which is to say a pageantlike presentation in which actors present to the audience a prepared monologue complete with all the Funny Voices. And they call the Funny Voices emotional preparation.

In life there is no emotional preparation for loss, grief, surprise, betrayal, discovery; and there is none onstage either.

Forget the Funny Voices, pick up your cue, and speak out *even though* frightened.

I'M ON THE CORNER

The best advice one can give an aspiring artist is "Have something to fall back on." The merit of the instruction is this: those who adopt it spare themselves the rigor of the artistic life.

I was once at a marriage ceremony where the parties swore "to try to be faithful, to try to be considerate . . ." That marriage was, of course, doomed. Any worthwhile goal is difficult to accomplish. To say of it "I'll try" is to excuse oneself in advance. Those who respond to our requests with "I'll try" intend to deny us, and call on us to join in the hypocrisy—as if there were some merit in intending anything other than accomplishment.

Those with "something to fall back on" invariably fall back on it. They intended to all along. That is why they provided themselves with it. But those with no alternative see the world differently. The old story has the mother say to the sea captain, "Take special care of my son, he cannot swim," to which the captain responds, "Well, then, he'd better stay in the boat."

————

The most charming of theories holds that someone other than Shakespeare wrote Shakespeare's plays—that he was of too low a state, and of insufficient education. But where in the wide history of the world do we find art created by the excessively wealthy, powerful, or educated?

It is not folly to ascribe the *oeuvre* to the unlettered, but it certainly is so to ascribe it to the nobility, whose entire lives were, to torture the conceit, "something to fall back on." It is both comfortable and prudent to have a fall-back position; and those possessing the happy same cannot help but have their work colored by it—such work must be more rational, considered, and possessed of the communitarian virtues than that of an outsider. Such prudent work would tend to shun conflict . . . well, you get my drift.

The other side of the coin is pride. One could say, "I am a fool, for I have not provided myself with an alternative"; one could also say, "I see nothing else worth my time," which is, I think, a rather strengthening attitude.

The cops say, "I'm on the corner." Young folks in the

theatre might have it, "Molly can go home and John can go home, I am *never* going home." Bravo. And good luck.

Those of you with nothing to fall back on, you will find, *are* home.

BUSINESS IS BUSINESS

T he prospectors of the Old West were in the mining business whether they knew it or not because they enjoyed the life of the outdoors. None of us is going to take it with us when we go, and all of us are going to go; and the prospectors, had you put them in a room which had billions of dollars of gold in it, and told them the gold was theirs, would they have been happy or sad? Or had they been given everything that that billion dollars could buy, would they have been content, or would they have longed to be back in the wilds with their burro, so to speak?

It's the same with the quest for fame and recognition. Certainly the drive for them is real. But let us exercise a bit of philosophy.

We'd all like to be thought well of, to do noble things, to do great things, and to be respected. But is it worthy of respect to act in a manner we ourselves feel trivial, exploitative, demeaning, or sordid? How can that command the respect of others; and would we value the approval of someone who is taken in by behavior which we know to be shoddy, grasping, and mercantile?

And yet our truly noble desire to do good work, to contribute to the community, becomes warped into an empty quest for something which we call success—that quest where many of you and many of your peers will squander your youth, your simplicity, and whatever you may have of talent—that quest in which you might be sitting for literally years in the outside offices of some casting agent begging for a role in a trivial manipulative piece of what is finally advertising and may not even be entertaining advertising at that.

An actor friend of mine moved to L.A. and did not work for three or four years. One day I asked how he was, and he told me he was angry, as he had just spent the day waiting to audition for a walk-on in a car-crash movie.

"Why don't you come back east," I said, "and work in the theatre."

"Hey," he said, "this is where the work is." He was a fine, respected, working actor. He situated himself in the midst of those he despised and chose to suffer their displeasure.

Do you desire the good opinion of these people? Are not these the same people you told me yesterday were fools and charlatans? Do you then desire the good opinion of fools and charlatans? That is the question asked by Epictetus.

And so we might ask ourselves, you and I, what is character? Someone says character is the external life of the person onstage, the way that that person moves or stands or holds a handkerchief, or their mannerisms. But that person onstage is *you*. It is not a construct you are free to amend or mold. It's you. It is *your* character which you take onstage.

The word "character" in the theatre has no other meaning. The ability to act, to resist, to assent, to assert, to proclaim, to support, to deny, to bear. These are the components of character onstage or off.

Your character, onstage or off, is molded by the decisions you make: which play you do, whether or not to pursue employment in commercials, in sex films or pseudo–sex films, in violent or demeaning films, in second-rate movies or plays; whether or not to treat yourself with sufficient respect to perfect your voice and body, whether or not to prepare for your scene, for your play, for your film, for your audition. Whether or not to conduct your business affairs circumspectly. The ideas, organizations, actions, and people you support and dedicate yourself to, mold and finally *are* your character. Any other definition is the jabbering of the uncommitted.

Certainly the weak would like you to believe that character is a costume which can be put on or taken off at will. And from time to time we'd all like to believe it. But that doesn't make it true.

You can pursue fame, but that doesn't mean that you will achieve fame, or that if you get it you'll find it is what you thought it was. Similarly, you can pursue money, or the phantom called mobility, which is to say, "I just want to get far enough ahead so that I can do whatever I want." Well, you can *attempt* whatever you want *today*, and if you can't today you aren't going to be able to tomorrow.

An actor who had moved to Los Angeles was once offered the lead in a play we were doing in Chicago, a lovely actor who was perfect for the role, and he said, "I'd love to be able to come and play the part, and I wish my career were far enough along to allow me to do so." That actor, like many of his brothers and sisters, sat alone home by the phone in L.A. for the eight weeks he could have been playing a part in Chicago. A part he professed that he'd love to play.

"If not now, when?" That's the question Hillel asked.

And if you like the theatre and the life of the theatre, participate in it like the prospector out there with his or her burro. *Participate* in it.

Yes, but sometimes of course we must decide to fill up the larder, or to make a less than perfect choice which might improve our chances to fill up the larder, you say. Granted. But which times are those, and on what basis do we choose? The Stoics would say, "Act first to desire your own good opinion."

That is the meaning of character.

Here is the best acting advice I know. And when I am moved by a genius performance, this is what I see the actor doing: *Invent nothing, deny nothing.* This is the meaning of character.

I've heard young actors speak of "stepping out." They felt constrained by the above suggestions, and they wanted, finally, a "part to tear a cat in," in which they could strut their stuff. They wanted to invent, to mold, to elaborate, to influence, to be a "transformational actor"—to be, in effect, anything but themselves.

No doubt, for the grass is always greener. But the so-attractive actions listed above are the work of the *writer.* It is the writer's job to make the play interesting. It is the *actor's* job to make the performance truthful.

When the performance is made truthful, the work of the writer is made something more than words on the page, not by the inventiveness, but by the *courage* of the actor. Yes, it might seem like a good, and might seem an attractive idea to embellish—it's your job to *resist* that attractive idea; for you cannot both "guide" the performance, and keep your attention and will on accomplishing your objective onstage. The impulse to "help it along," to add a bit of "emotion" or "behavior" is a good signpost—it means you are being offered—in resisting it—the possibility of greatness. *Invent nothing. Deny nothing.* Develop *that* hard habit.

It takes great strength of character—which is formed only over time and in frightening times—to

make difficult, and many times upsetting, decisions. Act
first to desire your own good opinion of yourself.

————

Today's vast amusement parks, "theme parks," offer not
amusement but the possibility of amusement. Like the
lottery, which offers not money but the possibility of
money. Similar is the academic/serfdom/great-chain-
of-being paradigm from which our current western system derives. We are trying to please the teacher, to get
into the good undergraduate school, to get into the
good graduate school, to get into the good postgraduate
program, to get into the good job.

The actor strives to please the panel, to get into the
good professional studio, to please the casting director,
please the agent, please the critic, and so progress. "But
progress to *what?*" I ask you.

These schematic, arithmetical models, while reas-
suring, are false. To serve in the real theatre, one needs
to be able to please the audience and the audience only.
This has nothing to do with the great chain of being, or
the academic model. The opinion of teachers and
peers is skewed, and too much time spent earning their
good opinion unfits one for a life upon the stage. By the
time one is twenty-eight years old and has spent twenty-
three of those years in a school of some sort, one is ba-
sically unfit to work onstage as an actor. For one has
spent most of one's life learning to be obedient and po-

lite. Let me be impolite: most teachers of acting are frauds, and their schools offer nothing other than the right to consider oneself part of the theatre.

Students, of course, do need a place to develop. That place is upon the stage. Such a model can and probably will be more painful than a life spent in the studios. But it will instruct.

And it is probably finally kinder to the audience to subject them to untutored exuberance than to lifeless and baseless confidence.

AUDITIONS

The audition process selects for the most blatant (and not even the most attractive) of the supplicants. As a hiring tool, it is geared to reject all but the hackneyed, the stock, the predictable—in short, the counterfeit.

The casting agent, and, to the largest extent, the talent agent are unacknowledged adjuncts of the production companies and studios. They reason, and in their place you or I might reason similarly, that the actors come and go but the producers go on forever.

The producers are not interested in discovering the new. Who in their right mind would bet twenty million dollars on an untried actor? They want the old—and if they cannot have it, they want its facsimile.

These gatekeepers understand their job to be this: to supply the appropriate, predictable actor for the part. They base their choice on the actor's appearance, credits, and quote—as if they were hiring a plumber.

If this sounds tedious, reflect that the actor himself is habituated into the process and endorses it from his first experience of it. And his first experience is the school.

The acting school and its lessons are many times harsh, but their rigor and extent is comfortable and predictable. The lessons of the stage, on the other hand, are often devastating and almost beyond bearing.

The school, like the audition process, has a clear and simple structure of commands and rewards. If, and as long as, the student propitiates the teacher, she may be disappointed but she will rarely be humiliated. To the extent that she internalizes her subscription to the system ("It is harsh, but I know in my heart it is just, or, at the very least, unavoidable") she can enjoy freedom from anomie. If she never ventures out of the confines of the system, she can live, whether employed or unemployed, free from terror.

Teachers of "audition technique" counsel actors to consider the audition itself the performance, and to gear all one's hopes and aspirations not toward the actual practice of one's craft (which takes place in front of an audience or a camera), but toward the possibility of appealing to some functionary. What could be more awful?

For much of the beauty of the theatre, and much of the happiness, is in a communion with the audience. The audience comes to the show prepared to respond as a communal unit. They come prepared (and expecting) to be surprised and delighted. They are not only willing, but disposed to endorse the unusual, the honest, the piquant. Everything the audition process discards.

Sitting in the auditorium, the audience learns not only—and perhaps not even primarily—from the stage but from one another. We all have had the experience of rehearsing a comedy, of seeing a joke fail there, only to see it later bring down a full house. The members of the audience are informed by and gain enthusiasms from one another—they come to be delighted, and to share that delight with one another.

The talent agent, the casting agent, the producer, sits in a room not to be entertained but to be judgmental. He or she sees the supplicant actor not as a friend bringing potential delight, but as a robber whose lack of skill, looks, or credits is going to deplete the precious coffers of the listener's time. It is a terrible process, and we learn to subscribe to it in school.

The worst result of this oppression, of this false vision of our role as actors, is that we internalize it. How often have we heard, and how often have we said, on leaving a performance, rehearsal, or audition, "I was terrible. . . . Oh, Lord, I was awful. . . ."

What is wrong with this? One might think it is a legitimate expression of the wish to improve. But it is not. It is an expression of the wish to have pleased authority. And in these cases where the authority is absent (or, in fact, congratulatory), we elect ourselves the stern taskmaster, and beat ourselves.

Why? Because we are taught, in fraudulent schools, by exploitative "agents" and directors, that we can please only by being abject and subservient to their authority. "There are ten thousand more where you came from, and if you are not correct in your attitude, not only will you not get the part [the place in the class] but you will not even be granted an *audition* to get the part."

Does this attitude seem familiar?

If we believe these schools, agents, and directors, we, over time, internalize and *become* that "bad parent," and curse ourselves.

As a member of the audience, I will tell you, it is an insult to come backstage and say to the performer, "You were great tonight," only to be told, "No, I was terrible. You should have seen me *last* week. . . ." Any of us who have been so corrected know that it feels like a slap in the face. Reflection would inform the actor that the correct response is "Thank you very much." The audience didn't come to watch a *lesson* but to see a play. If they enjoyed it, you, the actor, have done your job.

But suppose you learned something onstage, and that something will instruct or impel you to do something differently at your next performance. Well, one would hope that you learned something onstage. If you are a dedicated actor, dedicated to self-improvement, you *will* learn something. Sometimes that lesson will be simple and easy (I should not eat a meal so close to a performance), sometimes it will be momentous (My voice is a disgrace and I should retire from the stage till

I've fixed it), sometimes it will be life-changing (I am in
the wrong company, perhaps the wrong profession).
Any of these (and the gradients in between) can be
acted upon. *None* will be acted upon that find their expression in self-castigating or self-loathing.

Such remarks as "I am a fraud, I am no good, I
was terrible tonight" are the opposite of effective self-
improvement. They are obeisance to an outside or in-
ternalized authority—they are a plea to that authority
for pity for your helpless state.

But you are not helpless. You are entitled to learn
and to improve and to vary. (Is it rational that each of,
say, one hundred performances of a play should be, in
all respects, equal?)

You will not please either yourself or others in every
aspect of every outing. I have watched long runs over
the years, and have heard actors say "Tonight was fine"
or "Tonight was atrocious" of performances in which I
could find no difference. And I'm speaking of plays
which I wrote and directed, and in which I had a great
stake—plays and performances I would have improved
if I could have. Generally the "I'm garbage" and the
"I'm brilliant" performances were the same.

Does this mean the actor is psychotic for feeling a
difference? No. Some nights we feel better than others.
But the actor is wrong to invest such feeling with magical significance.

The purpose of the performance is to communicate

the play to the audience. If we bear this in mind, we will
be less likely to go around berating ourselves. This is a
habit caused not by *aesthetic,* but by *economic,* conditions.

There are many people trying to get into the theatre.
Stage and screen cannot contain all of them, so some
become teachers, agents, casting people, and most of
these (just as most actors) seek the real or imagined security of a hierarchical system: "I'm just trying to do
my job and to please my employers."

But the actor does not have employers. The agent
and the casting person are not employers, they are,
frankly, impediments standing between the actor and
the audience. Does that mean they should be ignored?
Well, many times they cannot be. There they are. But
they, and their job, should be kept in perspective.

One does not have to "like" them, and no amount of
toadying will induce them to like *us.* Again, the Stoics
say: "Do you want the respect of these people? Are they
not the same folk you told me yesterday were idiots and
fools? Do you then want the good opinion of idiots and
fools?"

Remember it.

Don't "confess" when you come offstage. If you
have gained an insight, *use* it. They say "silence builds a
fence for wisdom." To keep one's own counsel is difficult. "Oh, how terrible I was. . . ." How difficult to keep
those words in—how comforting they are. In saying
them one creates an imaginary group interested in

one's progress. But give up the comfort of an imaginary group. This "group" that is judging you is not real; you invented it to make yourself feel less alone.

I knew a man who went to Hollywood and languished jobless for a period of years. A talented actor. And he got no work. He came back at the end of the period and lamented, "I would have been all right if they'd just sat me down on day one and explained the rules."

Well, so would we all. But who are "they"? And what are the rules? There *is* no "they," and there are no rules. He posited the existence of a rational hierarchical group acting in a reasonable manner.

But show business is and has always been a depraved carnival. Just as it attracts the dedicated, it attracts the rapacious and exploitative, and these parasites can never be pleased, they can only be submitted to. But why would one want to submit to them?

The audience, on the other hand, *can* be pleased. They come to the show to be pleased, and they *will* be pleased by the honest, the straightforward, the unusual, the intuitive—all those things, in short, which dismay both the teacher and the casting agent.

Keep your wits about you. It is not necessary to barter your talent, your self-esteem, and your youth for the *chance* of pleasing your inferiors. It is more frightening *but it is not less productive* to go your own way, to form your own theatre company, to write and stage your *own* plays, to make your *own* films. You have an enormously

greater chance of eventually presenting yourself to, and
eventually appealing to, an audience by striking out on
your own, by making your *own* plays and films, than by
submitting to the industrial model of the school and
studio.

But how will you act when you, whether occasion-
ally or frequently, come up against the gatekeepers?

Why not do the best you can, see them as, if you
will, an inevitable and preexisting condition, like ants at
a picnic, and shrug and enjoy yourself in spite of them.

Do not internalize the industrial model. You are not one of
the myriad of interchangeable pieces, but a unique human being, and if you've got something to say, *say* it,
and think well of yourself while you're learning to say it
better.

PAINT BY NUMBERS

The only reason to rehearse is to learn to perform the play.

It is not to "explore the meaning of the play"—the play, for the actor, *has* no meaning beyond its performance. It is not to "investigate the life of the character." There is no character. There are just lines on the page.

A play can be rehearsed quickly, by a group of competent actors who know the lines, and are prepared, with the help of the director, to find the simple actions associated with them and to be arranged into an appropriate stage picture. If this is so, why squander months in rehearsal and years in school? The reason is economic.

Acting has become a profession of amateurs, a profession of the genteel class, and, by approbation, infinitely expansible. If one need not be employed to call oneself an actor, any number can play; and so "acting" becomes a refuge for the energy and time of the privileged class, like tatting or good works.

Since there is little chance of the vast hordes of amateurs being tested in performance, their "skills" need not be demonstrably useful. They are never to be used. So these "skills," capable of demanding the maximum of devotion, are the amateur's friend, since, in their endless study, one can stay and play and never be tested.

I remember a billboard on a Nevada road advertising some new slot machines at a casino. The sign read BIGGER PAY MEANS LONGER PLAY and was the most truthful piece of advertising I've ever seen. "We admit," the sign meant, "you do not gamble to win. We announce, in fact, that, as you know, you *will* not win. But we offer you more of that for which you gamble: gambling time."

The use to which the gambler puts his or her money is "time at the tables." And the use to which the acting student puts his or her time, money, and faith is "time at the school." It is an end in itself.

This hobby caste creates not only acolytes but their inevitable companions, priests. The priest caste—the teachers, coaches, managers, etc.—minister to those involved in this "work." But life in the studio, in "auditioning" classes, in casting offices, is not the work of acting. Acting is bringing the play to the audience.

How can it be learned? Perhaps it cannot. Perhaps

one can but perfect a disposition. Perhaps it must be
studied but cannot be taught. It has no point beyond
bringing the play to the audience.

The paint-by-numbers mechanical actor judges
himself and his performance constantly, and by a pre-
ordained checklist, as if acting were like rallye driving
and the actor rated by how accurately he hit each
checkpoint. And so the audience is robbed of any immediacy, and intimacy, of the unforeseen, of those few
things, in short, those sole things capable of rendering a
performance of a play superior to a reading of the text.

American schools of acting grew, in the main, from
a tradition of acting as a hobby. These schools teach
and reward those habits of thought and behavior which
fit the student for the leisurely life of the studio, and unfit them for any chance encounter they might have with
the real life of the stage—which is to say, with the audience.

The paint-by-numbers analysis of emotion memory,
sense memory, character dissection, and so on, is designed for the hobbyist who can take the piece apart at
her leisure with never a thought of performance. Its
merit is in its potentially endless consumption of time.

Actors must be trained to speak well, easily, and dis-
tinctively, to move well and decisively, to stand relaxedly,
to observe and act upon the simple, mechanical actions
called for by the text. Any play can then be rehearsed in
a few weeks at most.

"WORK"

The "work" you do "on the script" will make no difference. That work has already been done by a person with a different job title than yours. That person is the author. The lines written for you should be said clearly so that the audience can hear and understand them. Any meaning past that supplied by the author will come from your *intention toward the person to whom they are said.*

"Good day," on- or offstage, can be an invitation, a dismissal, an apology, a rebuke; it can mean anything, in short. Its meaning will come from the intention of the speaker toward the spoken-to. Similarly, onstage, a line's "meaning" *to the audience* is conveyed immeasurably quicker than, with more finality and force than, and, finally, supplants, any intention at explanation or embellishment on the part of the actor—it is conveyed by the actor's intention.

55

The tradition of oral interpretation, text interpretation, etc., may be all well and good for those addicted to the pleasures of the English Department, but these jolly disciplines have nothing whatever to do with the interchange between actor and audience. The audience perceives only what the actor wants to do to the other actor. If the speaker wants to do *nothing* to or about the other actor but wants only to interpret the text, the audience loses interest in the play. Such a performance at the amateur end of the scale is called stupid and stodgy; at the critically acclaimed end of the food chain, it is called Great Acting, which differs from acting, in the main, by being polite and predictable.

All the "connections" an actor makes between parts of a text are made to fill the time and mind of one with a little too much leisure. If the actor learned the lines and went on that night without the "textual work," the performance would only improve drastically. The work on the text, finally, shields the actor both from anxiety about his performance and from the necessity of paying attention to his colleagues while onstage.

The watchful, inventive, wary, cunning, brash individual nature intended for the stage is supplanted, in the text-analyzer, by the academic. Who wants to watch that person on the stage?

All of us have had the experience of the teacher who both bores and *knows* that he bores. "Yes," he says, "this material may be *boring*, but I Have Done the Work,

and I sentence you to hear it." The actor who devotes
herself to a fuller understanding of the textual significance of Madame Ranyevskaya's references to "Paris"
does similarly. Those connections have or have not been
made by the author. The author's contribution is the
text. If it's good, it doesn't need your help. If it's lacking,
there's nothing you can do to aid it. Recognize the fact
and learn to live with it—*the words and their meaning are not
your responsibility.* Wisdom lies in doing *your* job and getting on with it.

Here, again, is your job: learn the lines, find a simple
objective like that indicated by the author, speak the
lines clearly in an attempt to achieve that objective. Text
analysis is simply another attempt by the amateur to
gain admittance to our pubs.

Now let us be earnest and sincere and pretend for a
moment that a great desire to perform good works is
equal to artistic merit. This is the error of those who invest time endeavoring to "believe." It is not necessary to
believe anything in order to act. This delusion is attractive because and only because it allows the deluded to
"work hard."

Historically, the artist has been reviled and feared
because his or her job has nothing to do with hard
work. There's nothing you or I could do to enable us to
paint like Caravaggio, or to skate like Wayne Gretsky.
We could work all day every day for millennia, and we
would never achieve that goal. But students are given to

believe that they will be able to act like Fill-in-the-Blank
if and when they master the impossible. If, for example,
they can just learn to "believe."

But we cannot control what we believe.

Religions and political creeds which degenerate in
that direction demand belief. They receive from their
adherents not belief (which cannot be controlled) but a
certain more-or-less well-meaning avowal of hypocrisy:
"I proclaim that I have mastered that over which I know
I have no control, that I am part of that brotherhood
which proclaims similarly, and that I am opposed to all
who do not so proclaim."

The strength of these groups is directly proportional
to the individual's knowledge of his own failure to fulfill
its goals—it is the individual's attempt to conceal his
shame which binds these groups together. This is the
grand adhesive of the acting school. It is the reason for
"the fourth wall." The so-called Fourth Wall is a con-
struction of someone afraid of the audience. Why
should we strive to convince ourselves of the patently
false?

There is not a wall between the actor and the audience. Such would defeat the very purpose of the theatre, which is communication and communion.

Respect for the audience is the foundation of all legitimate actor training—speak up, speak clearly, open
yourself out, relax your body, find a simple objective;
practice in these goals is practice in respect for the au-

dience, and, without respect for the audience, there is no respect for the theatre; there is only self-absorption.

The urge to "believe" grows from a feeling of individual worthlessness. The actor before the curtain, the soldier going into combat, the fighter into the arena, the athlete before the event, may have feelings of self-doubt, fear, or panic. These feelings will or will not appear, and no amount of "work on the self" can eradicate them.

The rational individual will, when the bell rings, go out there anyway to do the job she said she was going to do. This is called courage.

ORAL INTERPRETATION

A director calls and asks, "You have a character in the script say 'I've been in Germany for some years.' Exactly how many years would that be?" It seems a legitimate question, and, indeed, it is. It is a legitimate desire to know how to play the scene. But the legitimate answer is "I can't help you."

First, the playwright does not know "how many years." The play is a fantasy, it is not a history. The playwright is not *withholding* information, he is *supplying* all the information he knows, which is to say, all the information that is germane. "The character" did not spend any time *at all* in Germany. He never was *in* Germany. There *is* no character, there are just black marks on a white page—it is a line of dialogue.

An actual person who said he had been in Germany would be able to answer the question "For how long?" *You* are an actual person, but the character is just a sketch, a few lines on the page; and to wonder of the character "How many years might he have spent in Germany?" is as pointless as to say of the subject of a portrait, "I wonder what underwear he has on?"

And no answer the questioner might receive could, finally, be acted upon. "I spent some years in Germany" cannot be acted differently than "I spent twenty years in Germany." It can only be *delivered* differently.

There is a school of theatrical thought which asks the player to, in effect, *interpret* each line and statement for the audience, as if the line were a word in a dictionary, and the actor's job was to perform the drawing which appeared next to it—to say the word "love" caressingly, the word "cold" as if shivering. This is not acting. It is Doing Funny Voices. It is the old Delsarte technique of the nineteenth century, come again to comfort us with its schematicism.

The Delsarte books of that bygone day showed photographs of the correct pose to adopt for each emotion and degree thereof: grief, mild grief, severe grief; diversion, amusement, hilarity, and so on. The responsible actor needed only to determine which emotion was required for each scene, and turn to the page indicated and Bob's your uncle.

The notion—art without the untidiness of uncertainty—survives, as this book suggests, in many forms, and one of them is oral interpretation. This is a high school event in which the competitor mounts the podium to embellish snippets of speech with age-old clichés of delivery.

It survives also in the "intellectual" school of script interpretation. "I want to know everything there is to know about this character and the times in which he lived," the actor says. "And if the author wrote, '. . . did smite the Sledded Polack on the Ice,' I want to know the crux of the dispute between Poland and Denmark which gave rise to that line, and I want to know the depth of the ice.'"

Sounds like a good idea. But it ain't going to help. It will not help you in the boxing ring to know the history of boxing, and it will not help you onstage to know the history of Denmark. It's just lines on a page, people. All the knowledge in the world of the Elizabethan era will not help you play Mary Stuart.

You have to learn the lines, look at the script *simply* to find a simple action for each scene, and then go out there and do your best to accomplish that action, and while you do, simply open your mouth and let the words come out however they will—as if they were gibberish, if you will.

For to you, to the actor, it is not the words which carry the meaning—it is the actions. Moment to moment and night to night the play will change, as you and your adversaries onstage change, as your conflicting actions butt up against each other. *That* play, *that* interchange, is drama. But the words are set and unchanging. Any worth in them was put there by the author. His or her job is done, and the best service you can do them is to *accept* the words *as is*, and speak them simply and clearly in an attempt to get what you want from the other actor. If you learn the words by rote, as if they were a phone book, and let them come out of your mouth without your interpretation, the audience will be well served.

Consider our friends the politicians. The politician who trots out the "reverent" parts of the speech "reverently," the "aggressive" parts "staunchly," the "emotional" parts "feelingly"—that person is a fraud, and nothing of what he or she would have you believe is true. How do we know we cannot trust them? We know because they are lying to you. Their very delivery is a lie. They have lied about what they feel in order to manipulate you.

We do not embellish those things we care deeply about.

Just as with the politician, the actor who puts on Funny Voices is a fraud. She may, granted, have a "good idea" about the script; but the audience isn't looking for a person with a "good idea" about the script. They are looking for a person who can *act*—who can bring to the script something they couldn't have learned or imagined from reading it in a library. The audience is looking for spontaneity, for *individuality*, for strength. They aren't going to get it from your tired old interpretive powers.

Here is what I have learned in a lifetime of playwriting: *It doesn't* matter *how you say the lines.* What matters is what you mean. What comes from the heart goes to the heart. The rest is Funny Voices.

HELPING THE PLAY

If it is necessary for us to devote the energy to believe that we are a Great Actor, or a character actor, or an ugly actor, or a charming actor, that energy will not be put into the task of observation and action on the things we have learned . . . let us accept ourselves and set about our task. If it is necessary for us to believe we live in turn-of-the-century Russia or that that woman who last week played our sister Anya is this week Arkadina our mother, that energy will not be devoted to getting our play done. All of acting, all parts, all seemingly emotion-laden scenes are capable of and must be reduced to simple physical actions calling neither for belief nor for "emotional preparation."

Most plays are better read than performed. Why? Because the feelings the play awakens as we read it are called forth by the truth of the uninflected interactions of the characters. Why are these interactions so less moving when staged by actors? Because they are no longer true. The words are the same, but the truth of the moment is cloyed by the preconceptions of the actors, "by feelings" derived in solitude and persisted in, in spite of the reality of the other actor.

An "intellectual" company of actors becomes a cabal of hypocrisy. "I will agree not to notice what you are truly doing, because to do so would interfere with my ability to trot out my well-prepared emotion at the appropriate instant. In return, you must agree not to notice what *I* am doing." So the investment in "emotion" makes the play not a moment-to-moment flow of the real life of the actor, but, instead, an arid desert of silly falsehoods enlivened periodically by a signpost of "fake" emotions.

But we need not hobble after false emotions. We are not empty. We are alive, and emotion and feeling flow through us constantly. They are not susceptible to our conscious mind, but they are there.

There is nothing we feel nothing about—ice cream, Yugoslavia, coffee, religion—and we do not have to add these feelings to a play. The author has already done that through the truth of the writing, and if he has not, it is too late.

Be a man; be a woman. Look at the world around you: onstage and off. Do not forsake your reason. Do not paternalize yourself. Your true creative powers lie in your imagination, which is eternally fertile, but cannot be forced, and your *will*, i.e., your true character, which can be developed through exercise.

To bring to the stage a mature man or woman capable of *decision based on will* is to make of acting not only an art but a *noble* art.

In so doing, you present to the eyes of a demoralized public the spectacle of a human being acting as she thinks right irrespective of the consequences. What is required is not the intellect to "help the play," but the wisdom to refrain.

ACCEPTANCE

Often, as students, we are struck with a sense of guilt because we cannot enter into that state of *belief* we think is required of us. We speak of "getting" the character. "Getting" the role. Of that magic time when we were onstage or in class and we somehow "forgot" that we were in a play or in a scene. And we feel that it is required of us to dwell always in this state, this magical state of psychosis: to dwell in a state where we "forget" that we are actors in a play and somehow "become" the characters. As if acting were not an art and a skill but only the ability to self-induce a delusional state.

But is this true of music? Does the musician devote his energies to forgetting that what is in front of him is a piano, and does the dancer strive to forget that she is dancing and endeavor to believe that what she is doing is walking?

This is why the ideas of substitution, sense memory, affective, or emotion, memory, are both harmful and useless: the idea is not to trick ourselves any more than it is to trick the audience; it is to *perform* something. What? The action of the play as set down by the author. Our job is the performance of that action as we discerned it in the text.

It is the choreography that we perform: the dancer does not endeavor to create either in himself or in the audience the *feelings* the choreography might evoke; he just performs the steps the most truthful way he knows how. Just so, our task is to execute the actions called for by the author. How, you ask, can we do so without *belief.* If we do not *believe* them, how can we *perform* them? Well, let's turn the attention outward.

Your belief is not the subject of the play. What could be less interesting? And if the task is uninteresting, your concentration will fall back on yourself. It *has* to. Why limit yourself? Choose something interesting to do.

Ever wonder what it would be like if your wife, husband, or lover died? Do you *believe* it has happened? No. You *imagine* for the moment that it has happened because it is enjoyable to do so. *Not to wish their death* but to *imagine.* To experiment with the dramatic.

Anyone ever play with the idea that you have a wasting disease, and you are writing your will? You toy with what you would say, with the wisdom you would impart from your position of one removed from life. . . .

What fun. Your imagination may, in fact, even be piqued by reading the above suggestion. Now: what happens to you when I ask you to *believe* you are dying?

————

The mind will always rebel at a direct command: fall asleep: fall in love: stop mourning: be interested. Relax. The command to *believe* will never be accepted by the mind, and all the supposed techniques to induce the capacity to believe do nothing other than take the "believer" away from the play and away from the idea of the play, away from the *fun* of the play. All of his energy becomes taken up in the precious shepherding and guarding of the *belief.*

"Can I see the flat? Can I see the audience? Are my fellow workers completely *costumed?* Can I 'see' the Fourth Wall?" So the believer falls into a false relation to the audience: the audience becomes an enemy capable of robbing the actor of his belief. On the other hand, play or dress-up, or imaginative fantasy, cannot be harmed by the presence of the "real." Why? Because they have a worth of their own. And what is that worth? We enjoy them.

————

To act means to perform an action, to *do* something. *To believe* means to hold a belief.

What are our beliefs in life? What do you believe?
Basic things. Things beyond your control. What would
it take to *change* one of those beliefs? To inculcate a new
one? Beliefs are unreasoning. In life, our beliefs are so
primordial, so basic, most times we don't even know
what they are. Let us leave belief alone. Let us deal with
something which *is* susceptible to reason.

Let us learn *acceptance*. This is one of the greatest
tools an actor can have. The capacity to accept: to wish
things to happen as they do. It is the root of all happiness in life, and it is the root of wisdom for an actor. Acceptance. Because the capacity to *accept* derives from the
will and the will is the source of character. Applying our
intention to use only one meaning for words, character
is the same onstage and off. It is habitual action.

Onstage or off, one may or may not believe that
one's father has died when faced with the facts. One can
strive to *accept* that fact: and that struggle is, of course,
the struggle of Hamlet. One may not believe that one's
wife has been unfaithful, but one may strive to *accept* it,
and so we have Othello; or that one's protégé has been
duplicitous and so we have *American Buffalo*.

The habit of cheerful acceptance is an aide in the
greater life in the theatre, too, because it induces truthful consideration: "The world is as it is, what can I do
about it?" But *belief,* on the other hand, induces self-
deception—e.g., I believe my teachers are bright, producers are powerful/evil/good, my director hates
me/loves me, the audience is good/bad/hot/cold.

Perhaps no one in a situation demanding courage (that is, in a situation that has frightened him) can believe it—when the ramp comes down on the landing craft on D-Day, when the baby is ready to be born, when the time comes to address the court, or to plead with the spouse for a second chance, or to ask the bank for an extension—when the time comes, in short, to act, it becomes apparent to these people, as it should to you, that no one cares what you believe, and if you've got a goal to accomplish you'd best set about it. To deny nothing, invent nothing—accept everything, and get *on* with it.

THE REHEARSAL PROCESS

The rehearsal process, as practiced in this country, is a demonstration of waste, and by extension, of the gentlemanly nature of acting. For if it is waste, it is not work, and if it is not work, then we are not workers, and, perhaps, that's what "art" means.

We spend our three weeks gabbing about "the character," and spend the last week screaming and hoping for divine intercession, and none of it is in the least useful, and none of it is work.

What should happen in the rehearsal process? Two things.

1. The play should be blocked.

2. The actors should become acquainted with the actions they are going to perform.

What is an action? An action is an attempt to achieve a goal. Let me say it even more simply: an action is the attempt to accomplish something. Obviously, then, the chosen goal must be accomplishable. Here is a simple test: anything less capable of being accomplished than "open the window" is not and can't be an action.

You've heard directors and teachers by the gross tell you, "Come to grips with yourself," "Regain your self-esteem," "Use the space," and myriad other pretty phrases which they, and you, were surprised to find difficult to accomplish. They are not difficult. They are impossible. They don't mean anything. They are nonsense syllables, strung together by ourselves and others, and they mean "Damned if I know, and damned if I can admit it."

One is up there onstage *solely* to act out the play for the audience. The audience only wants to know what happens next. And what happens next is what you (the actor) *do.*

That action has always got to be simple. If it's not simple, it can't be accomplished. One was capable of freeing the 101st Airborne at the Battle of the Bulge; but we could not Win the Hearts and Minds of the Vietnamese, as the direction was meaningless. Of course we lost the war. We didn't have an objective.

We all know what it means to *truly* have an objective. To get him or her into bed, to get the job, to get out of mowing the lawn, to borrow the family car. We know what we want, and, therefore, we know whether we're getting closer to it or not, and we alter our plans accordingly. This is what makes a person with an objec-

tive *alive:* they have to take their attention off themselves
and put it on the person they want something from.

Each character in the play wants something. It is the
actor's job to reduce that something to its lowest common denominator and then act upon it. Hamlet wants
to find out what is rotten in the state of Denmark. An
actor might perhaps reason, "Oh, *I* get it—Hamlet is
trying to *restore order.*" Scene by scene the tools necessary
to restore order might be: to interrogate, to confront, to
negotiate, to review . . . you get the idea.

All of the above are simple physical *actable* objectives. They do not require preparation, they require
commitment—and it is this commitment which the rehearsal process is supposed to rehearse.

If the actor goes to rehearsal with a mind and spirit
dedicated to discover and perform the actions simply
and truthfully, she will take this spirit onstage *along with*
the discoveries. If the actor whiles away the rehearsal
process looking for some magic "character," or "emotion," he will take onstage that same unfortunate capacity for self-delusion and beg the audience to share it
with him.

THE PLAY AND THE SCENE

The correct unit of study is not the play; it is the scene. The action involved in the play, the through-line of the character, is always too general to admit of being healthily physical. You might say that Horatio's through-line in the play was *to help his mentor out of a vicious trap*. That's all very well, and not inaccurate, but it's not going to be overly useful in the first scene with the players.

Any through-line must involve the character, and as the character exists only on the page and as we exist on the stage, his actions are not going to be helpful to us except as *guideposts*. The character wants to help his mentor out of a vicious trap. How does the character do it in *this* scene? *By awaiting instructions*. Good. Now, that is all you, the actor, have to do in the scene. And when you do that, you are fulfilling your responsibility to the play. You do not have *to await instructions* in order to *help your mentor out of a vicious trap.* You simply have to await instructions. Carve the big tasks up into small tasks and perform these small tasks.

Your responsibility to the character is done when you've chosen a simple action for the scene. There *is* no arc of the play; there *is* no arc of the character. Those are terms invented by scholars. They do not exist. Choose a simple action for the scene, and *play the scene.* There will be others onstage for you to play it with, and they and your objective will take more than enough of your energy.

After you finish one scene, you will encounter another one, with its *own* task; the total of them is the play. If you play each scene, the play will be served. If you try to drag your knowledge of the play through each scene, you are ruining whatever the worth is of the playwright's design, and you are destroying your chances to succeed scene by scene.

The boxer has to fight one round at a time; the fight will unfold as it is going to. The boxer takes a simple plan into the ring, and then has to deal with the moment. So do you. The correct unit of application is the scene.

EMOTIONS

The attempt to manipulate another's feelings is blackmail. It is objectionable and creates hatred and hypocrisy. If one asked an honest worker or craftsperson, "What did you want your client to *feel* on receipt of your work," he would most likely be dumbfounded. He had set out not to create an emotion in the recipient but to create an object—a chair, a table, a personal-injury defense, a meal.

For craftspeople in the theatre to set out to manipulate the emotions of others is misguided, abusive, and useless. In the theatre, as outside it, we resent those who smile too warmly, who act overly friendly, or overly sad, or overly happy, who, in effect, *narrate* their own supposed emotional state. Why do we resent it? Because we feel, rightly, that it is being done only to bring about or to extort something from us we would be reluctant to give in return for an uninflected presentation.

Business should be conducted in an unemotional environment. Anyone who presents herself in a business situation as a "friend," and therefore exempt from the usual rigors and niceties of businesslike accountability, is taking and will continue to take advantage of you. The honest diner goes to the restaurant to have good food in pleasant circumstances. She does not require the waiter's friendship, and the question "Is everything okay?" rather than being a service, is both an intrusion and the extortion of a compliment. "Yes," we say in effect, "I will smile back at you to get you to go away."

The addition of "emotion" to a situation which does not organically create it is a lie. First of all, it is not emotion. It is a counterfeit of emotion, and it is cheap. The respectful waiter will not demean his clients or himself by smarmy smiles and false narrations of his pleasure. And neither should the self-respecting actor.

Can we not imagine that the waiter or waitress, after fifty or so renditions of the question "Is everything all right?" might find the necessity of asking it onerous, might find his or her smile a little fixed, and might, finally, feel put-upon? If the waitress truly cares about whether or not the diners are enjoying themselves, she has ample room for operation—she might observe them and might both heed and anticipate their needs and take it upon herself to improve their enjoyment of the experience.

The addition of supposed "emotion" to a performance is an attempt to buy off the audience. In so
doing, in playing the "happy" line "happy," and the
"sad" line "sad," the actor strives, unconsciously, to put
himself above criticism—to fulfill *absolutely* the requirements of the line, to "have done well." It is another example of the academic-serfdom model of the theatre.
The audience couldn't care less. They came to see the
play. If the play is good, all of that mugging going on
under the name of "emotional memory" will lessen
their enjoyment, and they'll probably go along with the
gag because the play works, and they will attribute
much of their enjoyment of the play to the brilliant performances. Why? Because *you extorted it out of them.*
Through your "hard work," through your "emotions."

The greatest performances are seldom noticed.
Why? Because they do not draw attention to themselves,
and do not seek to—like any real heroism, they are simple and unassuming, and seem to be a natural and inevitable outgrowth of the actor. They so fuse with the
actor that we accept them as other-than-art.

It was said of African-American sports figures and
entertainers that they had "natural ability." This was a
code of WASP America—a sop and an insult to greatness, which meant "They are shiftless and lazy and have
succeeded through a fluke." Similarly, the industrial-
serfdom model of art wants to both endorse and define
"hard work" as if and because such an endorsement

permits the speaker to believe that, given the time, she could have made a similar accomplishment.

Emotion memory and sense memory are paint-by-numbers. They perpetuate the academic fallacy that, yes, yes, inspiration, bravery, and invention are very well, but they are not quantifiable for the purposes of the university, and so, cannot be art. What nonsense. Acting, like any art, can be learned, finally, only in the arena.

One can read all one wants, and spend eternities in front of a blackboard with a tutor, but one is not going to learn to swim until one gets in the water—at which point the only "theory" which is going to be useful is that which keeps one's head up. Just so with acting. The job of the actor is to communicate the play to the audience, *not* to bother it with his or her good intentions and insights and epiphanies about the ways this or that character might use a handkerchief—these are the concerns of second-class minds. And the lessons of the audience disabuse all but the most fatuous of the desire to "help."

Acting is a physical art. It is close to the study of dance or of singing. It is not like the study of mechanical drawing or literature to which the academics would reduce it.

Let the politicians have their fixed smiles and their crocodile tears, let them be the unabashed promoters of their own capacity to feel. Let us be circumspect and say the words as simply as possible, in an attempt to accomplish a goal like that delineated by the author— and then both our successes and our failures can have dignity.

ACTION

When you tell a joke, your choice of what to include and what to exclude relates solely to the *punchline of the joke*. Those things which tend toward the punchline are included; those things which are purely ornamental are excluded. One does this naturally, as one knows the punchline is the essential element. A joke holds our attention because we assume, as audience, that all elements presented to us are essential.

In a well-written play, and in a correctly performed play, everything tends also toward a punchline. That punchline, for the actor, is the *objective*, which means *"What do I want?"* If we learn to think solely in terms of the objective, all concerns of *belief, feeling, emotion, characterization, substitution,* become irrelevant. It is not that we "forget" them, but that something else becomes more important than they.

Take the joke: "A man goes into a whorehouse. A

run-down, weatherbeaten building nonetheless possessing a certain charm. Once, when the street was a residen-
tial block, the building, no doubt, housed a middle-class
family—a family with aspirations, trouble, and desires
not unlike our own. . . ." We see that all this, beautiful
though it may be, is irrelevant *to the joke*. Not irrelevant
in general, not *unbeautiful*, but irrelevant *to the joke*. What we
are being presented with may be a magnificent essay,
but we know it cannot be a joke, and that the teller is
misguided.

She wanted to "help."

How do we free ourselves from the misguided wish
to "help"? To free ourselves from having to decide
whether something is *effective, beautiful,* or *germane*, we
ask the question *"Is it essential to the* action?" and all else
follows. In so doing, we choose not to manipulate the
audience, *though we might*; we choose not to manipulate
the *script*, though we might; and we choose not to manipulate *ourselves*, though we might; and we find, by so
doing, that the audience, the script, and ourselves func-
tion better. What we are doing is eschewing *narration*. If
we devote ourselves to the *punchline*, all else becomes
clear.

The punchline is *the action*.

Think of it as a suitcase. How do you know what to
put in the suitcase? The answer is, you pack for where
you want to go.

———

Anyone can turn on a TV program fifteen minutes into
it and know exactly what is going on, and who did what
to whom. But television executives insist on including
fifteen minutes of narration in the script. Anyone can
look at a couple across the lobby of a hotel and tell
more or less what they are talking about and how they
feel about each other. You don't need narration in the
writing of a play, you need action. Just so, in the acting,
you don't need portrayal, you need *action.*

Again, what is this *action?* The commitment to
achieving a single goal. You don't have to become more
interesting, more sensitive, more talented, more obser-
vant—to act better. You *do* have to become more active.
Choose a good objective which is fun, and it will be
easy. Choose something that you *want to do.* The impulse
to *play,* to *imagine,* got you interested in theatre in the first
place. You knew, as children, that the game had to be
fun. You played "War" or "Marriage" or "Lost in the
Woods"—you did not play "Root Canal." Choose a fun
action. You remember how.

Actions rehearsed and performed grow stronger.
Because they are fun. You can rehearse that goodbye
speech to your girlfriend or boyfriend fifty times and it
is still fun. That's all the mystery there is to the "objective"—it is an action which is fun to do and is something like that which the author intended.

While you are intent on an *objective,* you do not have
to compare your progress to that of your peers, you do
not have to worry about a *career,* you do not have to

wonder if you are doing your job, you do not have to be *reverent* to the script—you are at work. Not only is it the simple solution to a seemingly complex problem, it is the right solution. Not only is it the right solution, it is the only solution.

GUILT

Any system built on belief functions through the operations of guilt and hypocrisy. Such a system, whether of acting training, meditation, self-improvement, etc., functions as a pseudo-religion, and is predicated on the individual's knowledge of his or her own worthlessness. The system holds itself out as the alleviator, cleanser, and redeemer of the guilty individual.

Now, none of us is free of self-doubt, and none of us is free of guilt. We all have thoughts, feelings, episodes, and tendencies which we would rather did not exist.

A guilt-based educational system, which is to say, most acting training, survives through the support of adherents *who were guilty before they signed up,* who came to classes and failed (how could they do otherwise, as the training was nonsense), and were then informed that their feelings of shame—which they brought *in* with them—were due to their failure in class, and could be alleviated if and only if the student worked harder and "believed" more.

Faced with nonsensical, impossible directions ("Feel the music with your arms and legs"; "Put yourself into the state you were in when your puppy died"; "Create a Fourth Wall between yourself and the audience"), the victim can choose one or both of the following choices: to strive guiltily to fulfill the demands, or to claim, falsely, that she has succeeded in doing so.

Both voices keep the student tied to the institution, the first out of guilt, and the second out of a (correct) apprehension: "I have succeeded here, but I fear my merit, like the soft currency of a bankrupt country, is dispensable only in these limited surroundings, and will not transfer to the outside world" (the stage).

Curiously, the state these systems profess to cure—anxiety, guilt, nervousness, self-consciousness, ambivalence—is the human condition (at least in the postindustrial age) and, coincidentally, the stuff of art. Nobody with a happy childhood ever went into show business. The states enumerated are what impelled you to go into the theatre in the first place. Psychoanalysis hasn't been able to cure them in a hundred years, and an acting school isn't going to cure them in two easy terms. They are part of life and they are part of our age and, again, they are at the *center* of not only your, but the universal, longing for drama.

You went into the theatre to get an explanation. That is why everyone goes into the theatre. The audience, just like you, came to have its anomie, anxiety, guilt, uncertainty, and disconnectedness dealt with. Your responsibility to them is this: deal with your own.

Your fear, your self-doubt, your vast confusion (you are facing an ancient mystery—drama—of course you're confused) do not *mar* you. At the risk of nicety, they *are* you. Sticking your head in the sand like an ostrich or an academician won't do the trick, if the trick is to bring the play to the audience.

What *will* do the trick? Well, as in any situation where one is lost, it is helpful to acknowledge one's state. We can say, "I'd be able to orient myself if I just knew where I was"; or "I'll go on a diet as soon as I've lost some weight"; or "I'll begin to *seriously* attempt to understand the art of the actor, and the requirements that art makes on me, as soon as I know what I'm doing."

When you accept that you *don't* know what you are doing, you put yourself in the same state as the protagonist in the play. Just like him, you are faced with a task whose solution is hidden from you. Just like the protagonist, you are confused, frightened, anxious. Just like him, your certainties will prove false, and humble you; you will be led down long paths and have to turn back; your rewards will come from unexpected quarters. This is the course of a play, a career, a performance, a life in the theatre.

Stanislavsky said that the job of the actor was to bring the life of the human soul to the stage. That life is *your* life. It is not neat and packaged. It is not predictable; it is often terrifying, disgusting, humiliating. It is all the things which make up your life. You don't have to wish it away. You *can't* wish it away, you can only re-press it. But you needn't do so.

The beginning of wisdom is the phrase "I don't under-stand." Fine. You are faced with a part, a play, a scene. Begin with the useful phrase "I don't under-stand." "I don't understand how I am to proceed." Per-haps you feel better already.

Let's revert to some very simple first principles: Your job is to communicate the play to the audience, by *doing something like* that which the playwright has shown the character to be doing. So, logically, a first step must be to observe what the character is doing.

At the beginning of *Hamlet,* Horatio comes onto the battlements to find out what all the hoopla is about this supposed ghost. That's what he's doing. There is no be-lief required, no emotion, only action. He, Horatio, wants to find out what the fuss is about.

All right. That's the *character.* The character is not *you,* it is not *anybody,* it exists only in the lines of dialogue on the page. What, then, are *you* to do? *You* don't want to do anything which involves a ghost, that would entail a certain measure of *belief* on your part. (What if you don't believe in ghosts, or don't believe in ghosts on the night of performance?)

Well, then, the next step of your task is to discard anything in the operations of the character which would require you to "feel" or to "believe"—to reduce the operations of the character to the lowest common denominator, so as not to burden yourself, so as to be able to act truthfully.

Now, you *might* or *might not* be able to act truthfully in a scene where you had to find out about a ghost; but nothing could stop you from acting truthfully in a situation where you had to *clean up a mess.*

One could say that that is the irreducible essence of that scene. (Please note that there may be other correct answers, but there is no *perfect* answer. It is the purpose of this simple analysis to get you out onstage playing a scene *something like* that which the playwright delineated. The search for the *perfect* analysis will keep you *off* the stage and in the classroom.) So, you say that, in the scene, *your* job is to *clean up a mess.* (Horatio's job was to clear up the hoopla about the ghost; *your* job is to clean up a mess.) Please note that we have, at this point, left Shakespeare's scene behind. We need never again refer to the ghost, or to fear, or to belief. The purpose of our simple analysis is to understand not the *appearance* but the *mechanics* of the scene. We want to lift up the hood, as it were, and look at the wiring.

All right. Now, when we go to a party, we are introduced to many people. Some we have met before, but we remember them vaguely. It is helpful, in these cases, to ask a friend, "Who is that woman again?" And the friend might respond, "Oh, she's the wildlife veterinarian," and we nod, and, our recollection jogged, we say, "Oh, yes. Thank you."

Similarly, when we have determined our action (in this case, to clean up a mess), we might require or enjoy a jog to our memory: "*What* does that mean again?" This is where the application of the phrase "as if" becomes most helpful. *What* does it mean to clean up a mess?

Well, it's as if you went shopping with your little sister and she was caught shoplifting. And you go to the store manager and clean up her mess. It's as if the credit card company charged you three thousand dollars for items you never bought. You don't have to *believe* these things have happened. First, it's impossible, as they didn't happen. They are fantasy; and, second, even if you did "believe" them, it wouldn't aid you in playing the scene. They, these "as ifs," are just *reminders*, should you need them, to help you clarify to yourself the action in the scene.

The action in this scene, remember, is to clean up a mess. That is the action, or the objective, you have elected in this scene. You no more have to feel like, or even *think* about, "My little sister has been caught shoplifting" than you have to feel like a sick horse when you meet the veterinarian.

You have, in this simple analysis, used your powers of reason and of application to discover a simple, actable goal for yourself, which is *something like* that which the playwright devised for the character. The work you have done to arrive at such a goal has given you not only understanding but confidence, as you have applied yourself to things you can control.

Because you have increased both your understanding and your confidence, you are less likely to be confounded or humiliated by an ignorant or arrogant director, or casting agent, should you encounter same. You have made a *choice* and, in so doing, have put yourself in the same situation as the protagonist.

Horatio does not exist. But, *if* he existed, he, on the battlements, might feel fear of the ghost, might feel himself unprepared to quell the fears of Marcellus and Bernardo, *might* curse the fate which had elected him their military superior and, so, responsible for the situation.

You *do* exist. When you are up—in an exposed position—not upon the battlements, but upon the stage—*you* might also feel unprepared, might feel you have made the wrong choice of an objective or of a career, might feel unequal to the task, might feel loathing for your fellow players.

Everything you ever feel onstage will be engendered by the scene. In rejecting a situation based on guilt (I can do *more*, do *better*, find a perfect solution, and, so, avoid uncertainty), in beginning with a frank avowal (I am confused, uncertain, and full of self-doubt), and proceeding honestly from one step to the next, you put yourself in the same position as the written character and can begin to bring to the stage the truth of the moment: *your* fear, uncertainty, self-doubt, courage, confidence, hardiness; yourself, in short, and your art.

CONCENTRATION

There is a fashionable pediatric diagnosis going around these days called attention deficit disorder. A friend remarked, "What a thing—in my day it used to be called daydreaming."

Now you, like everyone else, daydream. You dream of fame and fortune, of triumphal accomplishments and terrible misfortunes; you have, in short, an active, imaginative mind. You don't have a very well developed power of what you have learned to call "concentration," and the good news is that you don't need it. For acting has nothing whatever to do with concentration. Perhaps you have read and studied and pondered Stanislavsky's "circle of concentration," in which you were asked to now enlarge, now constrain, your concentration, now to the room, now to the tabletop, now to your wristwatch, and so on.

I know you have also done such exercises as the

"mirror game" and have practiced concentrating on a past incident, feeling, or emotion, all with greater or lesser success.

But success and failure in the above are equally irrelevant. Acting has nothing to do with the ability to concentrate. It has to do with the ability to *imagine*. For concentration, like emotion, like belief, cannot be forced. It cannot be controlled.

Try this exercise: concentrate on your wristwatch.

How did you do? Your ability to force your concentration lasted the briefest fraction of a second, after which you thought, "How long can I keep this up?" or, alternatively, "How interesting this all is, look how the hands go around!" which was, let us confess, hypocrisy—there was nothing interesting about it at all; you forced yourself to "concentrate," and the result was falsity and self-loathing, as it, inevitably, must have been. For concentration cannot be forced.

Your concentration is like water. It will always seek its own level—it will always flow to the most interesting thing around. The baby will take the cardboard box over the present it contained, and as Freud said, a man with a toothache can't be in love. A new pack of cigarettes might be important if one has not had one for a month, but interest in it might pale before a first intimate encounter with a new partner, interest in which would fade next to the death of a parent, which would be of importance secondary to escape from a burning building.

Interest or investment in one's own powers of concentration is, finally, just another rendition of self-absorption and, as such, is a complete bore. The more you are concerned with yourself, the less you are worthy of note.

The more a person's concentration is outward, the more naturally interesting that person becomes. As Brecht said: Nothing in life is as interesting as a man trying to get a knot out of his shoelace.

The person with attention directed outward becomes various and provocative. The person endeavoring to become various and provocative is stolid and unmoving. We've all seen the "vivacious" person at the party. What could be a bigger bore? It's not your responsibility to do things in an interesting manner—to become interesting. You are interesting. It's your responsibility to become outward-directed. Why not direct yourself toward the actions of the play? If they are concrete, provocative, and fun, it will be no task at all to do them; and to *do* them is more interesting than to *concentrate* on them.

Concentration cannot be forced. It is a survival mechanism and an adaptive mechanism, and it will not stand down and stop making its own connections simply because we'd like it to. Acting, finally, has nothing whatever to do with the ability to concentrate. The ability to concentrate flows naturally from the ability to choose something interesting. Choose something legitimately interesting to do and concentration is not a problem. Choose something less than interesting and concentration is impossible.

The teenager who wants the car, the child who wants to stay up an extra half hour, the young person who wants to have sex with his or her date, the gambler at the racetrack—these individuals have no problem concentrating. Elect something to do which is physical and fun to do, and concentration ceases to be an issue.

If it's not physical, it can't be done (one can wait, but one cannot "improve the morals of a minor"); if it's not fun, it won't be done. (One can "suggest methods of self-improvement," but one wouldn't want to do it; on the other hand, the same objective might be restated actively, and we'd find it easy to "tell off a fool.")

Choose those actions, choose those plays, which make concentration beside the point. Believe me, if concentration is an issue for you, it will be one for the audience. When you choose the play you are burning to do, you will, likely, choose those actions and objectives within the play which are similarly fun. You not only have a right to choose actions which are fun, you have a responsibility—that's your job as an actor.

Here is a bit of heresy: Our theatre is clogged with plays about Important Issues; playwrights and directors harangue us with right-thinking views on many topics of the day. But these are, finally, harangues, they aren't drama, and they aren't fun to do. The audience and the actor nod in acquiescence, and go to their seats or go onstage happy to be a right-thinking individual, but it is a corruption of the theatrical exchange.

The audience should go out front and you should go

onstage as if to a hot date, not as if to give blood. No one wants to pay good money and irreplaceable time to watch you be responsible. They want to watch you be exciting. And you can't be exciting if you're not excited; and you can't be excited if you're thinking about nothing more compelling than your boring old concentration, self-performance, and good ideas.

A friend once had dinner with Margaret Thatcher and reported, "You know, I couldn't believe it myself, but there's something sexy about her." And I'm sure there was. She was gadding about, at the top of her game, having her own way, plotting, scheming, commanding. What did he find sexy? Power.

Exercise your own power in your choice. Make a compelling choice and it's no trick to commit yourself to it. "Concentration" is not an issue.

TALENT

Aconcern with one's talent is like a concern with one's height—it is an attempt to appropriate prerogatives which the gods have already exercised.

I am not sure I know what talent is. I have seen moments, and performances, of genius in folks I had dismissed for years as hacks. I've watched students of my own and of others persevere year after year when everyone but themselves knew their efforts were a pitiful waste, and have seen these people blossom into superb actors. And, time and again, I saw the Star of the Class, the Observed of all Observers, move into the greater world and lack the capacity to continue.

I don't know what talent is, and, frankly, I don't care. I do not think it is the actor's job to be interesting. I think that is the job of the script. I think it is the actor's job to be truthful and brave—both qualities which can be developed and exercised through the will.

An actor's concern with talent is like a gambler's concern with luck. Luck, if there is such a thing, is either going to favor everyone equally or going to exhibit a preference for the *prepared.* When I was young, I had a teacher who said that everyone, in the course of a twenty-year career, was going to get the same breaks—some at the beginning, some at the end. I second and endorse his observation as true. "Luck," in one's business dealings, and "talent," its equivalent onstage, seem to reward those with an active and practicable philosophy.

The Pretty Girl or Boy will grow old, the "sensitive sophomore" will have to grow up or pay the consequences, the wheel will turn, and hard work and perseverance *will* be rewarded. But a concern with talent is a low-level prayer to be rewarded for what you now are.

If you work to improve those things about yourself which you may control, you will find you have rewarded *yourself* for what you have become. Work on your voice so that you may speak clearly and distinctly although wrought-up, frightened, unsure, overcome (the audience paid to hear the play); work on your body to make it strong and supple, so that emotion and anxiety do not contort it unpleasantly; learn to read a script to ferret out the action—to read it not as the audience does, or as an English professor does, but as one whose job is to bring it to the audience. (It's not your job to *explain* it but to *perform* it.) Learn to ask: What does the character in the script want? What does he or she do to get it? What is that like in my experience?

Pursuit of these disciplines will make you strong and give you self-respect—you will have worked for them and no one can take that from you. Pleasure in your "talent" can (and will) be taken from you by the merest inattention of the person on whom you have deigned to exercise it.

A common sign in a boxing gym: BOXERS ARE OR-DINARY MEN WITH EXTRAORDINARY DETERMINATION. I would rather be able to consider myself in that way than to consider myself one of the "talented"; and—if I may—I think you would, too.

HABIT

We tend to repeat those things we have repeated. It's not especially laziness; it's just the way we are constructed. It is the way our mind works. How can we use this propensity to our advantage? By *habitually* performing the tasks of our craft in the same way.

In the theatre, as in other endeavors, correctness in the small is the key to correctness in the large. Show up fifteen minutes early. Know your lines cold. Choose a good, fun, physical objective. Bring to rehearsal and to performance those things you will need and leave the rest behind.

You can also cultivate the habit of wiping your feet at the door. We all know we should do this when we enter the theatre door, but we should also do this when we leave.

Leave the concerns of the street on the street. And when you leave the theatre, leave that performance behind you. It's over—if there is something you want to do differently next time, *do* it.

Put things in their proper place. Rehearsal is the time for work. Home is the time for reflection. The stage is the time for action. Compartmentalize and cultivate that habit and you will find your performances incline to take on the tinge of action.

Be generous to others. *Everyone* tries to do the best he or she can. Take the beam from your own eye. There is certainly something you can correct or improve in yourself today—over which you have control. That habit will make you strong. Yearning to correct or amend something in someone else will make you petty.

Cultivate the habit of only having aversion for those things you can avoid (those things in yourself) and only desiring those things you can give yourself. Improve yourself.

An actor is, primarily, a philosopher. A philosopher of acting. And the audience understands him as such.

People, though they may not know it, come to the theatre to hear the truth and celebrate it with each other. Though they are continually disappointed, the urge is so inbred and primal they still come. Your task is to tell the truth. It's a high calling. Cultivate the habit of pride in your accomplishments, large and small. To prepare a scene, to be punctual, to refrain from criticism, to learn your lines cold—these are all accomplishments, and while you pursue them, you are learning a trade, a most valuable trade.

You bring onstage the same thing you bring into a room: the person you are. Your strength, your weakness, your capacity for action. Dealing with things as they are strengthens your point of view. A *most* valuable possession for an actor.

Cultivate a love of skill. Learn theatrical skills. They will give you continual pleasure, self-confidence, and link you to fifty thousand years of the history of our profession.

Singing, voice, dance, juggling, tap, magic, tumbling. Practice in them will perfectly define for you the difference between possession and nonpossession of a skill. If you do these things, you will begin to cultivate the habit of humility, which means peace. A person who has done her job that day has fulfilled her responsibilities and pleased God. That person can sleep well.

Cultivate the habit of mutuality. Create with your peers, and you are building a true theatre. When you desire and strive to rise *from* the ranks rather than *with* the ranks, you are creating divisiveness and loneliness in yourself, in the theatre, and in the world. All things come in their time.

Cultivate the habit of truth in yourself.

In choosing the stage, you offer yourself constantly to the opinion of others. Mediocre minds must, of necessity, have mediocre ideas of what constitutes greatness. Consider the source.

Be your own best friend and the ally of your peers, and you may, in fact, *become* that person, that friend, that preceptor, that benefactor you have always wished to encounter.

That is not a *character* onstage. It is *you* onstage. Everything you are. Nothing can be hidden. Finally, nothing can be hidden in *any* aspect of your life. When we say Lincoln had character, we do not mean the way he held a cigarette. When you say your grandmother had character, you do not mean the way she used a hanky. If you have character, your work will have character. It will have *your* character. The character to do your exercises every day over the years creates the strength of character to form your own theatre rather than go to Hollywood; to act the truth of the moment when the audience would rather not hear it; to stand up for the play, the theatre, the life you would like to lead. There is nothing more pragmatic than idealism.

THE DESIGNATED HITTER

Disneyland is a rather restrictive work environment. The behavior of its employees is strictly prescribed and monitored. Individuality and improvisation are not, in the main, encouraged. But there is a counterexample.

I visited Disneyland in 1955, and again in 1995, and on both visits witnessed this deviation: the men who "ran" the boats on the Jungle ride delivered a patter, which, while mild in the extreme, contained a touch of welcome institutional self-mockery. Further, the boat drivers were the wee-est bit free to improvise—to depart from the prepared script in a vein mildly mocking of the institution. It was there at the park's opening in 1995, and use and forty years' custom had ingrained it—a *droit de fou*, or fool's license, to mock the dictatorial stolidity of the Establishment.

Similarly, the concierge at many London hotels enjoys a position to some degree licensed to banter, to gossip, perhaps to camp—in short, to familiarize with the patrons, and so mitigate an unpleasant aspect of all that institutional propriety. And there are other examples of a position part of the duties of which are to mock, or at least mitigate, the dignity of the institution: the high school shop teacher and the television weather man are two. The hospital nurse, her visit coming on the heels of that of the hospital doctor, is another. And it's noteworthy, I think, that the *quality* of their performance in these socially designated roles, is unimportant. It is the existence of the roles which delights us—that and the willingness of the actors to fulfill them. We do not require brilliance in the performance, merely willingness.

Similarly, there is a spontaneously occurring position in the acting profession. It is that of the Great Actor. This is, in effect, an honorary position, awarded from a cultural need for the place to be filled, and not according to the merit of the individual. Indeed there is little or no merit required from the person so designated, save the willingness (whether in awe or vanity) to go along with the gag.

Truly great performances cause us to question, to pause, to ponder, to reexamine. They do not conduce to the immediate ejaculation "bravo"; and so the Great Actor is, of necessity, seldom a very good actor. We praise his or her performances as we would praise our own possessions if we could do so with impunity. That is the gift of the Great Actor, and the reason he is so well rewarded—he allows us to act vainly and call it gracious appreciation. It is an example of our cultural insecurity. The praise means "Yes, and by God, he's *mine. I've* got one, too."

We delight to slather appreciation on this place-holder for the minor inconvenience it causes us. It allows us to feel we have paid for the right to consider ourselves aesthetic. Our praises are as the sneezes of the fellow with a summer cold who enjoys informing us that it was caused by the air conditioner in his new car. We praise the Great Actor for all the world as if we were lauding the fiscal brilliance of the treasurer of the United States. And, like that honorary post, that of the Great Actor seems perpetually filled—one dies and another appears as if by parthenogenesis. We must require him. And we do. His presence reassures us that we need not be moved by art.

Victorian physicians cautioned women to avoid at all cost that phenomenon they called "spasmodic trans-ports" (orgasm), as nothing could be worse for the health. In our rote adulation of the Great Actor we instruct and remind ourselves to shun the spontaneous, the antisocial, the innovative, the organic. It is an inversion of the *droit de fou.*

Well, propriety is fine in its place. But its place is not in the theatre. The theatre belongs not to the great but to the brash. And it is our job as theatre people to point out—both in comedy and in tragedy—the folly of the whole thing. We are not there to celebrate the status quo, or our capacity to celebrate—that is the job of the

cocktail party, the banquet, and the political conven-
tion. Our job is and should be that of professional de-
tractor.

The profession of the Great Actor, on the other
hand, is that of Dig-No-Ty. The Great Actor is the human equivalent of the Cow Pageant at some worthy
livestock fair—his job is to attempt to add the imprimatur of artistic immediacy to the essentially self-
serving. The position might seem to be a bargain, but
nobody ever enjoyed that pageant; they only pretended
to because of its cost.

PERFORMANCE AND CHARACTER

The preoccupation of today's actor with character is simply a modern rendition of an age-old preoccupation with *performance,* which is to say, with oneself. It is, in every age, the old lookout of the ham actor.

To ask constantly of oneself "How'm I doing?" is no more laudable or productive than to ask it of the audience. When we do so, we pander to a supposed magical, mythical "perfection" and, in so doing, abdicate our responsibility to tell the story simply. Such is not acting. It is, again, self-advertisement and posturing, and is best left to those who think that an imaginary future good justifies lying.

Whether or not lying in general is a justifiable offense is a question for moral philosophers. Onstage it is *never* justified. Better to miss a laugh, an "emotional oasis," a moment, a beat, than to add an iota to the "performance" in order to make sure the audience "understands." They came to see a play, not your reasoned "emotional" schematic of what your idea of a character might feel like in circumstances outlined by the play.

Finally, a concern with the "arc of the play" or the "unity of the character" is only a concern with performance. It is the desire to act perfectly, and so escape censure. But such escape is not to be found onstage. You are as apt to be censured for brilliance as for incompetence. And the notion that more emotional and sensory preparation is going to win over those in authority is as bootless as the idea that if you get better grades Daddy will stop drinking.

If you decide to be an actor, stick to your decision. The folks you meet in supposed positions of authority—critics, teachers, casting directors—will, in the main, be your intellectual and moral inferiors. They will lack your imagination, which is why they became bureaucrats rather than artists; and they will lack your fortitude, having elected institutional support over a life of self-reliance. They spend their lives learning lessons very different from the ones you learn, and many or most of them will envy you and this envy will express itself as contempt. It's a cheap trick of unhappy people, and if you understand it for what it is, you need not adopt or be overly saddened by their view of you. It is the view of the folks on the verandah talking about the lazy slaves.

There is nothing contemptible in the effort to learn and to practice the art of the actor—irrespective of the success of such efforts—and anyone who suggests there is, who tries to control through scorn, contempt, condescension, and supposed (though undemonstrated) superior knowledge is a shameful exploiter.

A preoccupation with emotion memory, sense memory, the character, is only an attempt to placate this generic person, to identify with her, accept her prejudices as one's own.

The academic-bureaucratic model of the theatre—that put forward by the school and by the critics—presents itself as intellectual, but it has nothing to do with intelligence or culture; it is antiart; and in rejecting the innovative, the personal, the simple, and the unresearched, it rejects all but mob-acceptable pablum.

It has been written that it is easy to get the mob to agree with you—all you have to do is agree with the mob. An apprenticeship spent looking inward for supposed "emotion," while perhaps spent with honest motives, trains one only to be a gull. An actor should never be looking inward. He or she must keep the eyes open to see what the other actor is doing moment to moment, and to call it by its name and act accordingly. If one cannot do that onstage, it is unlikely one will be able to do it in the school, casting office, and so on.

To face the world is brave. To turn outward rather than inward and face the world which you would have to face in any case—such may not always win the day, but it will always allow you to live the day as an adult.

———

A word about teachers. Most of them are charlatans. Few of the exercises I have seen, in what were advertised as acting schools, teach anything other than gullibility. Don't leave your common sense at the door of an acting school. If you don't understand the teacher, make the teacher explain. If they are incapable of either explaining or demonstrating to your satisfaction the worth of their insights, they do not know what they're doing.

You can't live your life believing every ten-penny self-proclaimed teacher, critic, agent, etc., and then walk out onstage and be that model of probity and wisdom and strength you admire and wish to be. If you want that strength, you're going to have to work for it, and your first and most important tool is common sense.

THE VILLAIN AND THE HERO

All of us have had the experience of watching television and hearing the announcer say: "The assailant, twice convicted of aggravated assault, was serving a life sentence for manslaughter at the time of his escape. When the police engaged him in the gun battle, he turned his weapon on his hostages and opened fire." And as the announcer speaks, we see on the screen a photo of an intense, bearded man, and we say to ourselves, "Well of *course* that man is a criminal. How could anyone fail to notice it! Every line in his face proclaims him a depraved villain."

And, as we so muse, the announcer continues: "The photo you see depicts the heroic clergyman who dashed from the crowd, subdued the gunman, and saved the lives of all the hostages." And then: "Oh," you say to yourself. "Oh. I see it now. Of course. Look at that determination. Look at that simple, steady resolve—obviously the face of a hero. Anyone could see it."

You've done it, I've done it, we've all done it. It is not that we are stupid but that we are suggestible. Let's learn the lesson: it is not the actor's job to portray.

The audience will accept anything they are not given a reason to disbelieve. Here is what I mean: a young woman across the room at a party is pointed out to us as being worth $500 million. We now begin to look at her a little differently. "Oh," we think, "*this* is how the Rich act. This is how they drink their tea or light their cigarettes. Aha. How *odd*. In many ways, just like you and me. . . ."

Just like the villain/clergyman in the news report, the young woman has done *nothing*. A characteristic was ascribed to her, and we accepted it. Why should we not?

We will continue to accept it until we are given a reason to disbelieve. What would be such a reason? If she, for example, produced a vast roll of bills and began distributing them.

But yet, such pointless clownishness is exactly that in which we indulge when we add "characterizations" to our performance.

The work of characterization has or has not been done by the author. It's not your job, and it's not your look-out.

You don't have to portray the hero or the villain. That's been done for you by the script.

ACTING "AS IF"

Read whole Chapter

Here's a phrase which appears in several languages, the French say *L'esprit de l'escalier*, in Yiddish it's *Trepverter*, both of which mean "What I *should* have said." We leave the room, and only then does the beautiful, effective, moving speech occur to us. And the speech *always* has an object: to bring the tyrant-employer low; to correct the vicious stepparent; to instruct the deficient; to eulogize the personal hero.

We act out these dramas not only in regard to actual personal events but also in regard to fantastical ones—that is, to those events we can participate in only through fantasy: we make the summation in the O. J. Simpson trial; we convince FDR to bomb the railroad tracks leading to Auschwitz; we defend Dreyfus or the Scottsboro boys, we personally congratulate Charles Lindbergh, or Neil Armstrong, or Nelson Mandela.

We perform these personal dramas for our audience of one all day long. They take no preparation; they need only description—you see the difference? As soon as we have named these dramas, we can play them. These lovely dreams do not require "preparation"—we do not "believe" we are meeting Mandela; we only act "as if" we were. It's like playing lacrosse. In order to play lacrosse you have to know the rules. The purpose of the rules is to make the game more enjoyable—you don't have to prepare or put yourself into a lacrosse state of mind.

These games, these fantasies, are highly dramatic and idiosyncratic. We enjoy them because in them we *act*—which means we perform them in order to achieve an objective—as above, to reveal the abuser to himself, to instruct the tyrant in simple humanity, to win the obstinate to common sense.

In none of these do we have to "remember" how we are supposed to feel. We simply remind ourselves what we are about to do, and we are suffused with the desire to *do* it: we jump immediately and happily into the midst of the game, we begin our harangue, our explanation, our apology, protest, summation. We can make our speech to the tyrant time after time, and indeed we do, sometimes improving it, sometimes simply repeating it for the joy it affords us.

Any method of acting—any interchange in life, for that matter—which is based upon the presence or absence of emotion sooner or later goes bad. We have all seen the perfectly good marriage discarded because one of the partners "fell out of love." The religious who has a crisis of faith is undergoing the inevitable and will do so periodically.

The actor does not need faith; and like the religious in the crisis, the actor is both called upon and *paid*, not to do the thing for which she is perfectly prepared, but to do that for which she is unprepared, unfitted, and which she would much rather avoid. This is called heroism.

Joan chooses to honor her voices over saving her life; Hamlet chooses to get to the bottom of a vile and sordid entanglement when everyone around him calls him mad to do so; Henry V, on the eve of a battle which will likely bring his death, chooses to make a speech to his comrades, not of extortion but of thanks—he pays a debt; Sonia chooses to devote herself to Uncle Vanya rather than wallow in her loss. This is drama. Human beings contending bravely with their fate, their circumstances, and their nature.

What do we say of the actor who would wish it all away—the immediacy, the ungainly bravery of people in extremes—who would wish it all away and substitute some shoddy counterfeit of emotion? We say that such a one is great, that he is a Great Actor, and that we have never seen such technique.

What does this talk of technique mean? It means we were so starved of anything enjoyable that we were reduced to enjoying our own ability to appreciate. What would the word "technique" mean if applied to a chef? Or a lover? It would mean that their works and actions were cold and empty and that, finally, we're disappointed by them. This is precisely what it means when applied to a performance onstage.

Most actors are terrified of their jobs. Not some, most. They don't know what to do, and it makes them crazed. They feel like frauds.

Failure offers, at the least, support for their worldview, but success, to them, is agony. That which makes the actor uncomfortable—and I speak from observation as actor, director, teacher, and writer—that which makes the actor uncomfortable is *always* the scene. He and she, when unschooled, will attribute it to deficiencies in their preparation, in the preparation or attitude of their colleagues, to deficiencies in the script, and say or portray "I just could not be comfortable doing that," and, in so saying, they are right.

But when, in our fantasies of saving France, defeating Hitler, pleading for Dreyfus or for woman's suffrage, are we ever comfortable? We may be *happy,* or enjoy, as we only can in fantasies, dolor and misery, but we are in a state of excitement-upset which has *nothing* to do with being comfortable.

The actor cannot distinguish the cause of his perturbation—nor should he. It's not his job. His job is to get out onstage and *act in spite of it.* In spite of *whatever* he's feeling. Henry V would rather be alone with his fears, and his reflections, but in spite of it he chooses to

pay a debt, in the St. Crispin's Day Speech. Clarence
Darrow would rather have leapt to his feet and cried,
"My opponent is a fool, and his arguments a fool's prat-
tle," but in spite of it he reasoned the judge through the
Scopes Monkey trial, the Leopold and Loeb case, and
so on. Jackie Robinson held his peace, and showed the
world true heroism by *not* expressing himself.

And *you* can show the audience some heroism.
That's why they came to the theatre. They didn't come
to see "technique," whatever *that* may be.

You are going to bring your unpreparedness, your
insecurities, your insufficiency to the stage whatever you
do. When you step onstage, they come with you. Go onstage and act in spite of them. Nothing you do can
conceal them. Nor *should* they be concealed. There is
nothing ignoble about honest sweat, you don't have to
drench it in cheap scent.

And when you go onstage determined *to act*, that is,
to get what you came for, and not to be denied, you can
come offstage at peace.

There is nothing more pointless or more common
than the spectacle of the actor coming off, going home
head hung, saying to herself and her colleagues, "I was
not good tonight. I failed."

Leave it onstage. If your objective is only to do a
good performance, the feeling of failure can only cast
you into an anxious fugue state of self-consciousness. If,
on the other hand, you come onstage to get something
concrete from the other person, a feeling in any one

moment of failure can and should and will only ener-
gize you to try harder.

"Technique" is the occupation of a second-rate
mind. Act as you would in your fantasy. Give yourself a
simple goal onstage, and go on to accomplish it bravely.

That dedication is up to you. Everything else is with
the gods.

"THEY ONCE WALKED AMONG US"

The prestige of most acting teachers rests upon the idea of apostolic succession.

They advertise that they studied with the students who studied with the students, who, at the beginning of the chain, studied with one of the great. Now, the great are safely dead and cannot be quizzed, but we might assume that they brought something of passion and courage to their work—that they were assured of nothing other than their own dissatisfaction with the status quo. It was the force, logic, or romance of their vision that emboldened students to reject conventionally approved approaches and throw in their lot with the newcomer.

These originals had no dogma, no imprimatur to fall back on. And if their vision and instruction did not please or divert or instruct, if it was not practical, the students left.

As we progress further down the chain, both the students and the teachers are attracted not to the *new* but to the *approved*.

It is not the iconoclast who enters the equation at this point but the academic or hobbyist—that person looking for stability. Certainly, most of us have learned something from a teacher. But I doubt if anyone ever learned anything from an Educator. I suggest that the piety we find in these Schools of the Annointed is institutionalized ancestor worship, in which the absent ancestor stands in for our infinite perfectability, i.e., if we strive and strive and strive, we might be able to attain to the clean perfection of Those Who Once Walked Among Us. Yet those ancestors were no more perfect than we—they were unsure and brash and arrogant and wrong and right as the rest of us.

That they managed, in spite of their human frailty, to assert their view sufficiently to found a school and attract followers might inspire us—but instead of inspiring us to worship their shades, it might inspire us to found our own schools.

ELEVEN O'CLOCK ALWAYS COMES

One discovers one's old friend, the jeune premier playing the kindly old doctor. Well, *that* went quickly.

Here is an exchange from Chekhov:

ASTROV: We find that *this*, that we are *living*, is our life.

VANYA: . . . it is?

ASTROV: Quite.

It goes so quickly. You can pass your life waiting for a break—and it will pass in the blink of an eye.

The old joke has the fellow haranguing God, "Let me win the Lottery." The fellow goes on, days and months on end. "Just let me win the Lottery." And finally the heavens part, and a weary voice says, "Buy a ticket."

Your life in the theatre, like mine, will pass before you are aware of it. And you will realize why the old folks reminisce—it is not that they are nostalgic; they are stunned. It went so quickly.

We all would like to be part of, to create, that theatre which we could participate in with pride. On which we could reflect with pride. To do so, one has to buy a ticket. The price of admission is *choice*—the choice to participate in the low, the uncertain, the unproved, the unheralded, to bring the truth *of yourself* to the stage. Not the groomed, sure, "talented," approved person you are portraying; not the researched, corseted, paint-by-numbers presentation-without-flaws, not the Great Actor, but yourself—as uncertain, as unprepared, as confused as any of us are.

Art does not flourish in subsidy, and it does not flourish in the studio—it is more frightening, more sordid, funnier, and truer than the certainties of the instructor. It is the stuff of the soul. It is the counterbalance to the reasonable view of the world; and, so, it is likely to be despised.

To cherish, rather than despise it—that's the job of the artist.

MERITOCRACY

I prize my life as a member of a reviled profession.

I've been privileged to witness in a rehearsal room greatness of a magnitude and with a frequency seldom seen onstage. I've heard and seen things funnier and dearer at the crafts service table in the middle of a night-shoot than anything heard by anyone in any majority culture.

I've played cards with Roland Winters, who played Charlie Chan; I've shot pool with Neil Hamilton, who was in *The Informer*. I once walked across a room to introduce myself to what was obviously a very beautiful and slim young woman with astonishingly long red hair (I'd only seen her from the back), and when she turned, found myself speaking with Lillian Gish, and she talked to me, for a half hour, about Mr. Griffith.

I worked with Don Ameche, and he told me stories about growing up in his father's salon in Kenosha, Wisconsin. I did a play with José Ferrer—who was the world's greatest Cyrano—and another with Denholm Elliot, who took a bite of a plum and told me it reminded him of Sonja Henie's derrière.

I wrote my first film script for Bob Rafelson. His uncle, Samson Raphaelson, wrote *The Jazz Singer*, the first talkie, and gave me notes, through Bob, on *my* first screenplay.

Someone said, of the flight training of a U.S. Naval Aviator, that there was not enough money in the world to purchase it, it could be won only through merit. Similarly, advancement, subsistence, friendship, regard, in the theatre, is priceless to me and has been, after the love of my family, frankly, the guiding desire of my life: to win and keep a place in our culturally despised profession through merit.

I was fortunate to come up in the years when every performer entered show business through the stage. There was, when I was young, no writer, or actor, or director who began in television or in film. This meant that my friends and I learned—or were given the chance to learn—the use of the age-old barometer of theatrical merit: the audience. Did we think it funny? Well, did the audience laugh? Did we think it moving— did they sigh? Was the second-act curtain surprising— did they gasp? (A standing ovation can be extorted from the audience. A gasp cannot.)

I was fortunate to grow up in an environment that

made it easy to prefer the well-made to the shoddy. The well-made paid the rent.

The well-made play, scene, design, direction, the good performance, must be *true*. The simple truth may stem from a natural disposition, or come from years of arduous study—it's nobody's business but your own.

The blandishments of fame, money, and security are great. Sometimes they have to be quieted, sometimes they have to be compromised with—just as in any other sphere of life.

What is true, what is false, what is, finally, important?

It is not a sign of ignorance not to know the answers. But there is great merit in facing the questions.